New Testament Bible Story Patterns
(People, Places, Animals & Scenery)

by
Sherrill B. Flora

Cover and Inside Illustrations by
Julie F. Anderson

The Lord's Prayer

Our Father who art in heaven,
hallowed be thy name,
thy kingdom come,
thy will be done,
on earth as it is in heaven.
Give us this day our daily bread,
and forgive us our trespasses,
as we forgive those
who trespass against us,
and lead us not into temptation,
but deliver us from evil.
For thine is the kingdom
and the power and the glory
forever and ever. Amen

Publishers
In Celebration
a division of Instructional Fair • TS Denison
Grand Rapids, Michigan 49504

Standard Book Number: 1-56822-331-5
SPCN: 990-219-2610
UPC: 0 13587 22264
New Testament Bible Story Patterns – People, Places, Animals & Scenery
Copyright © 1996 by Instructional Fair • TS Denison
2400 Turner Avenue NW
Grand Rapids, Michigan 49504

HOW TO USE THE PATTERNS

New Testament Bible Story Patterns will help bring Bible stories to life for the children in your classroom, home, or church. The patterns have a wide variety of uses that will make your story telling or bulletin board displays easy-to-create, providing you with successful tools for teaching God's Word.

There are two different types of patterns:
PEOPLE AND ANIMALS
PLACES (Buildings) AND SCENERY

Here are some ways that you can use the patterns:

PEOPLE AND ANIMALS

- *Stick Puppets* – Copy the pattern, color the pattern, cut it out. Glue the pattern on tag board or posterboard. Laminate for durability. Tape to a tongue depressor or popsicle stick. The children may wish to make their own puppets to bring home. These can simply be made by coloring and cutting out each pattern and taping it to a stick.

- *Paper Bag Puppets* – Copy the pattern, color the pattern, cut it out. Glue the pattern on a lunch-size paper bag. The children can put their hands in the bags and use as hand puppets.

- *String Puppets* – Copy the pattern, color the pattern, cut it out. Cut a piece of string about 24" long. Fold a 3" x 5" index card in half. Place the string in the folded card and tape or glue the top edge of the card together. Attach the string to the puppet with tape. (Follow the illustration.)

- *Flannel Board Characters* – Copy the pattern, color the pattern, cut it out. Glue the pattern on tag board or posterboard and cut it out from the tag or posterboard. Laminate for durability. Attach a small piece of self-stick velcro, or glue a small piece of sandpaper to the back.

PLACES AND SCENERY

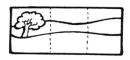

- *Puppet Stage* – Create a background board similar to the display board shown in the illustration. The scenery pages can be taped on the background board. String puppets (see above) work well with this type of puppet stage.

ADDITIONAL IDEAS FOR THE PATTERNS

Bulletin Board Displays – You can enlarge the patterns on a copy machine. Color, cut them out and staple to a bulletin board. They make wonderful large displays that the children can continually learn from and enjoy. It is even more fun to provide the children with the patterns and let them have the fun of creating the bulletin board.

Big Books – Make a classroom book of Bible stories. Provide the children with the characters, animals, buildings, scenery, etc., from a Bible story. Let the children color and cut out the patterns. Glue the patterns onto poster boards. Punch holes in the left-hand side of the posterboard. Bind together in book form. Add scripture underneath the pictures. Let the children enjoy retelling and "reading" their picture Bible Stories. Add a story to the book each time the children hear or learn a new Bible Story.

CONTENTS

The number in parentheses is the page number where the pattern can be found.

The number in parentheses is the page number where the pattern can be found.

The Stormy Boat Ride – *Matthew 8:18, 23-27; Mark 4:35-41; Luke 8:22-25*
Jesus and His Disciples in Boat, Storm (147-148), Calm Day (145-146)

Weakness of King Herod – *Matthew 14:1-12; Mark 6:14-29*
King Herod (35), Herodias (36), Herodias' Daughter (36), Inside of Home (159-160)

Jesus Teaching – *Matthew 14:13-15; Mark 6:30-36; Luke 9:10-12*
Jesus in a Boat (145-146), Hillside with Many People (137-139)

Food For Thousands – *Matthew 14:16-21; Mark 6:37-44; Luke 9:13-17; John 6:4-14*
Jesus (21), Group of Disciples (152), Little Boy (37), Food Baskets (38), Hillside with Many People (137-139)

Jesus Walks on Water – *Matthew 14:22-33; Mark 6:45-52; John 6:15-21*
Jesus (39), Peter (24), Boat in Storm (147-148)

The Transfiguration – *Matthew 17:1-9; Mark 9:2-10; Luke 9:28-36*
Moses/Jesus/Elijah Scene (41-42), Jesus (21), Group of Disciples (152)

The Greatest of Heaven – *Matthew 18:1-6; Mark 9:33-37; Luke 9:46-48*
Jesus Sitting (28), Small Children in Group (43), Group of Disciples (152)

Healing the Lepers – *Luke 17:11-19*
Jesus (21), 9 Lepers in Group (44), 1 Individual Leper (45), Desert Road Scene (121-122)

The Good Samaritan – *Luke 10:25-37*
Injured Man (46), Robbers (46 & 47), Religious Leader (47), Good Samaritan (48), Innkeeper (48), Donkey (101), Desert Road Scene (121-122)

Martha and Mary – *Luke 10:38-42*
Mary (49), Martha (49), Jesus Sitting (28), Inside of Home Scene (159-160)

The Good Shepherd – *Matthew 18:12-14; Luke 15:4-7*
Shepherd (11), Group of Sheep (102)

Lazarus Lives – *John 11:1-44*
Jesus (21), Mary (49), Martha (49) Lazarus (50), Group of Disciples (152)

The Prodigal Son – *Luke 15:11-32*
Father (51), Young ProdigalSon (50), Older Son (51), Desert Road Scene (121-122)

Let The Children Come – *Matthew 19:13-15; Mark 10:13-16; Luke 18:15-17*
Jesus (21), Group of Children (52), 2 Individual Children (53), Group of Disciples (152)

Zacchaeus – *Luke 19:1-10*
Zaccheus in Tree (53-54), Jesus (21), Happy Crowd Cheering (55), Group of Disciples (152)

Mary's Act of Love – *Matthew 26:6-13; Mark 14:3-9; John 12:1-8*
Jesus Sitting (28), Mary (49), Martha (49), Lazarus (49), Inside of Home (159-160)

Entry To Jerusalem – *Matthew 21:1-11; Mark 11:1-11; Luke 19:29-44; John 12:12-19*
Jesus on Donkey (56), People Lining Street with Palms (57-58), Happy Cheering Crowd (55), Group of Disciples (152)

Cleaning Out the Temple – *Matthew 21:12-16; Mark 11:15-18; Luke 19:45-48*
Jesus Angry (60), 2 Moneychangers (59), Blind Person (35), Crippled Person (34), Pharisees (23), Outside Front of Temple Scene (149-150)

Widow and the Penny – *Mark 12:41-44; Luke 21:1-4*
Jesus (28), Group of Disciples (152), Woman Holding a Baby (61), Inside of Temple Scene (117-118)

Five Foolish Bridesmaids – *Matthew 25:1-13*
5 Foolish Bridesmaids (62), 5 Wise Bridesmaids (63), Desert Road Scene (121-122), Outside Front of Temple Scene (149-150)

Judas Plots – *Matthew 26:1-5; 14-16; Mark 14:1-2; 10-11; Luke 22:1-6)*
Judas Iwith Silver (64), Chief Priests (64), Inside of Temple Scene (117-118)

The Last Supper – *Matthew 26:20-29; Mark 14:17-25; Luke 22:14-23; John 13:18-27*
The Last Supper Scene (65-67)

When the Cock Crows – *Matthew 26:31-35; Mark 14:27-31; Luke 22:31-34; John 13:31-38*
Jesus (40), Disciples (24, 25, 29, 30, 31, 32), Desert Road Scene (121-122)

Garden of Gethsemane – *Matthew 26:36-46; Mark 14:32-42; Luke 22:39-46; John 17:1-18:1*
Disciples Sleeping/Jesus Praying/ (68-69)

Betrayed by a Kiss – *Matthew 26:47-50; Mark 14:43-46; Luke 22:47-48; John 18:2-9*
Judas Kissing Jesus (70), 2 Soldiers (80), Religious Leaders Carrying Clubs (71), Desert Road Scene (121-122)

Peter Denies Jesus – *Matthew 26:58, 69-75; Mark 14:54, 66-72; Luke 22:54-62; John 18:15-18, 25-27*
Peter Sitting By Fire (72), First Girl (72), Peter Standing (24), Second Girl (73), Group of Men (73), Crow on Pedestal (107)

Jesus & Pilate – *Matthew 26:59-68; 27:1-2, 11-14; Mark 14:55-65, 15:1-5; Luke 22:63-23:5; John 18:19-24, 28-38*
Pilate on throne (74), Sad Jesus (74), Religious Leaders (71)

Herod and Jesus – *Luke 23: 6-12*
Herod (75) Jesus (74); 2 Soldiers (80); Angry Crowd (98), Inside Temple Scene (117-118)

Pilate Tries to Free Jesus – *Matthew 27:15-26; Mark 15:6-15; Luke 23:13-25; John 18:39-40*
Pilot (74), Jesus (74), Barabbas (75), Soldiers (80), Angry Crowd (98), Outside Front of Temple (149-150)

Cruelty to Jesus – *Matthew 27:27-33; Mark 15:16-22; Luke 23; 26-31; John 19:1-17*
Jesus with Crown of Thorns (76); Cross (76), Guards [make many] (80)

Jesus Crucified – *Matthew 27:34-50; Mark 15:23-37; Luke 23:34-46; John 19:18-30*
Jesus on the Cross (77), Criminals on Crosses (78), Women Crying (79), Group of Disciples (152), Crowd of People (89)

The Burial – *Matthew 27:54-60; Mark 15:39-46; Luke 23:49-54; John 19:38-42*
Open Tomb with Jesus Inside (153-154), Mary [Jesus' Mother] (81), Mary (81), Mary Magdalene (82)

Guarding the Tomb – *Matthew 27:61-66; Mark 15:47; Luke 23:55-56*
Guard (80), Religious Leaders (23), Pilate (74), Tomb with Boulder In front (155-156)

An Empty Tomb – *Matthew 28:1-8; Mark 16:1-8; Luke 24:1-10; John 20:1*
Mary [Jesus' Mother] (81), Mary (81), Mary Magdalene (82), Angel (82), Soldiers (80), Tomb with Boulder In Front (155-156)

Mary Magdalene Sees Jesus – *Mark 16:9-11; John 20:3-18*
Mary Magdalene (82), Risen Jesus (83), Group of Disciples (152)

The Disciples See Jesus – *Mark 16:14-16; Luke 24:36-48; John 20:19-21*
Risen Jesus (83), Inside of Home (159-160), Group of Disciples [cut out Thomas] (152)

Doubting Thomas – *John 20:24-29*
Group of Disciples [Cut out Thomas] (152), Thomas (31), Risen Jesus (83)

Breakfast at the Sea of Tiberias – *John 21:1-19*
Risen Jesus (83), Peter (24), 5 other Disciples (24, 30, 31), Fishing Boat (125-126)

Home to The Father – *Mark 16:19-20; Luke 24:50-53; John 14:1-2; Acts 1:3-11*
Jesus Ascending to Heaven (84), Group of Disciples (152)

Coming of the Holy Spirit – *Acts 2:1-13*
Disciples with the Flames of the Holy Spirit (85-86)

The Apostles Heal and Teach – *Acts 2:43-3:10*
Peter(24), John (29), Crippled Man (94), Healed Man (94)

Peter and John Arrested – *Acts 3:11-4:22*
Peter (24), John (29), Religious Leaders (23), Inside Prison Scene (123-124)

An Angel Frees the Apostles – *Acts 5:12-42*
Inside Prison with the Apostles (87), Angel (88), Priests (23), Inside Temple Scene (117-118)

Stephen Arrested/The First Martyr – *Acts 6:8-7:60*
Stephen (88), Angry Crowd (98), Outside Front of Temple (149-150)

Saul Becomes a Follower of the Lord – *Acts 8:1-4; Acts 9:1-8; 22:4-11; 26:9-18*
Saul (90), 2 Friends (90), Desert Road Scene (121-122)

Peter Visits Cornelius – *Acts 10:17-48*
Peter (91), Cornelius (91), Inside of Home (159-160)

Peter Escapes Prison – *Acts 12:1-17*
Angel (92), Peter (91), Guards (80,92), Inside of Home (159-160), Inside Prison Scene (123-124)

Saul Becomes Paul the Preacher – *Acts 9:10-25; 14:1-22*
Saul (93), Barnabas (93), Crippled man (94), Healed man (94), Outside Front of Temple (149-150)

Singing in Prison – *Acts 16:16-34*
Paul (95), Silas (95), Jailer (96), Paul and Silas Free (96), Inside Prison Scene (123-124)

Paul Speaks to An Angry Group – *Acts 21:27-23:11*
Older Paul (97), Commander (97), Angry Crowd (98), Soldiers (80); Outside Front of Temple (149-150)

Paul Before Agrippa – *Acts 25:1-26:32*
Paul (97), Festus (99), King Agrippa (99), Outside Front of Temple (149-150)

Shipwrecked – *Acts 27:1-44*
Shipwreck Scene (157-158)

Paul In Rome – *Acts 28:11-31*
Paul Writing Letters in Prison (100)

The number in parentheses is the page number where the pattern can be found.

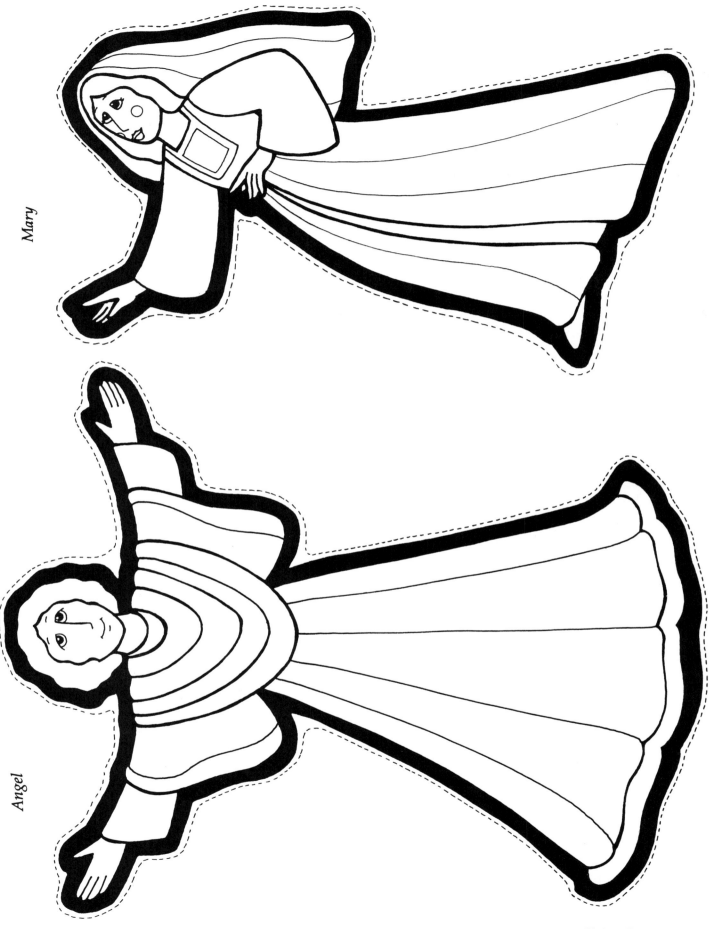

Mary

Angel

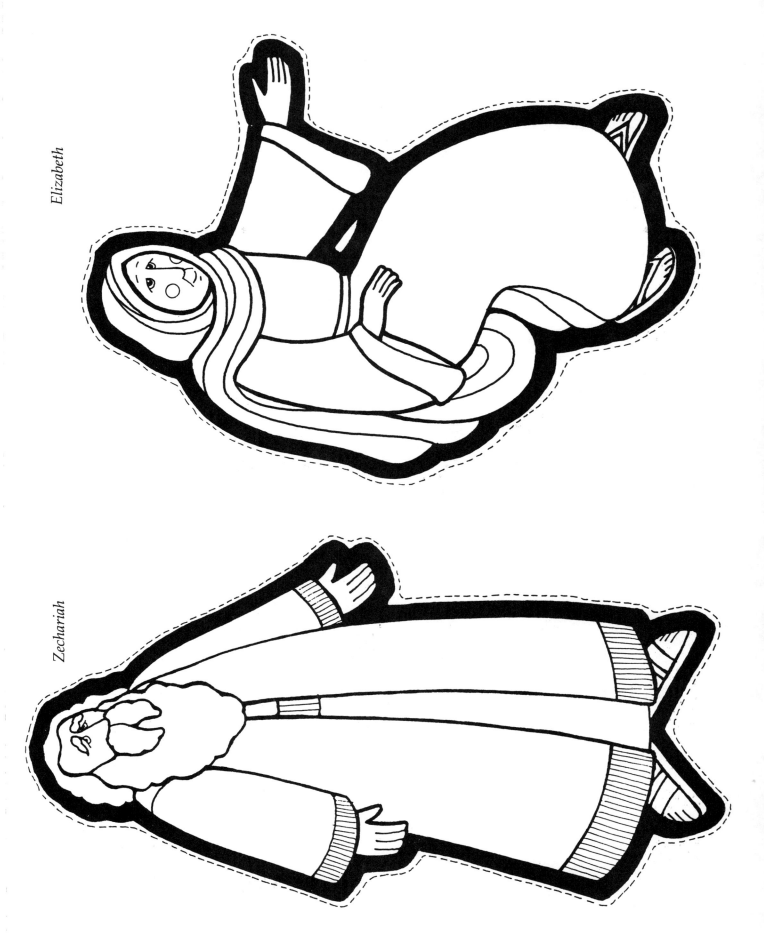

Elizabeth

Zechariah

Joseph

Innkeeper

Group of Shepherds

10

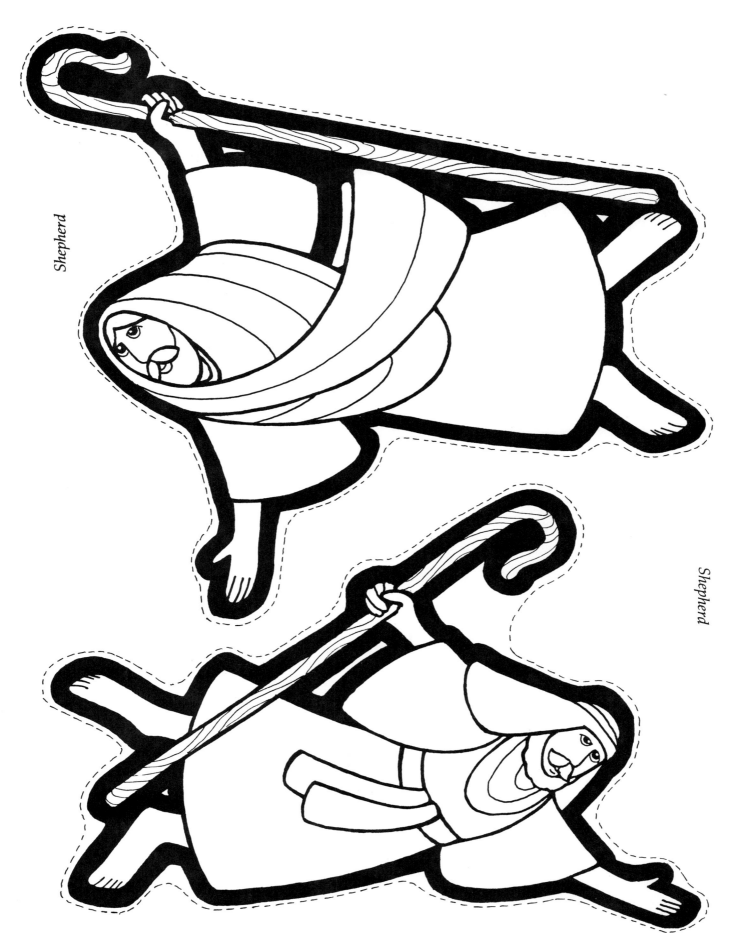

Shepherd

Shepherd

IF9699 New Testament Bible Story Patterns

Baby Jesus in Manger

Star

Mary Kneeling

Baby Jesus not in Manger

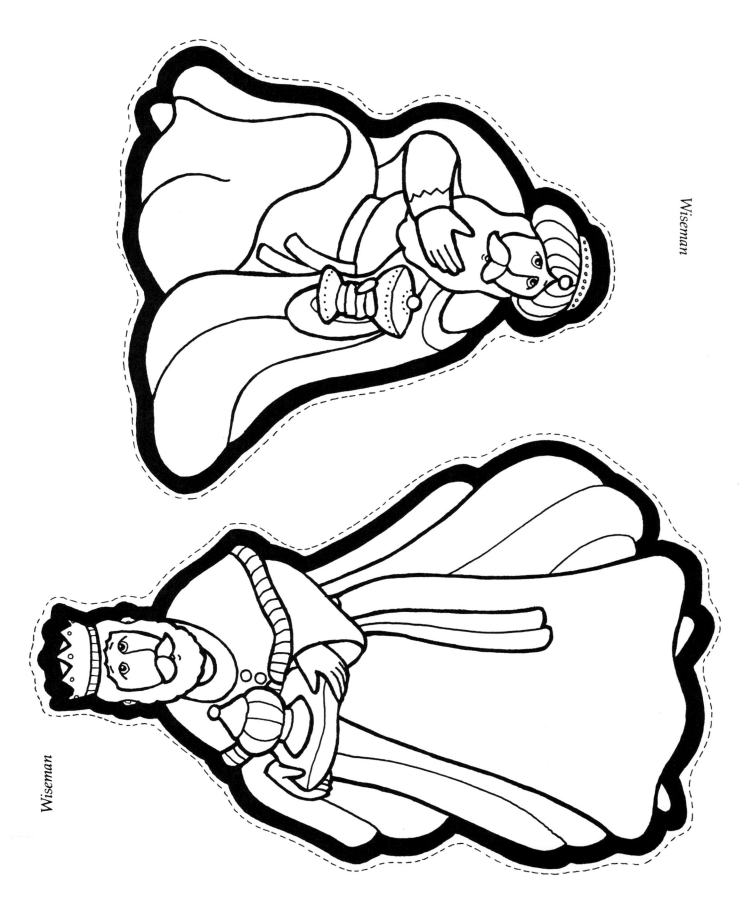

Wiseman

Wiseman

Jesus as a Small Child

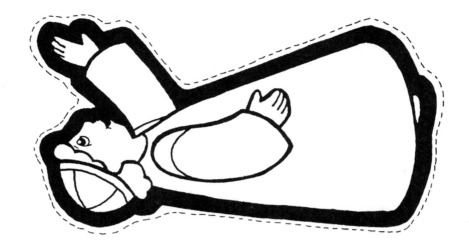

Wiseman

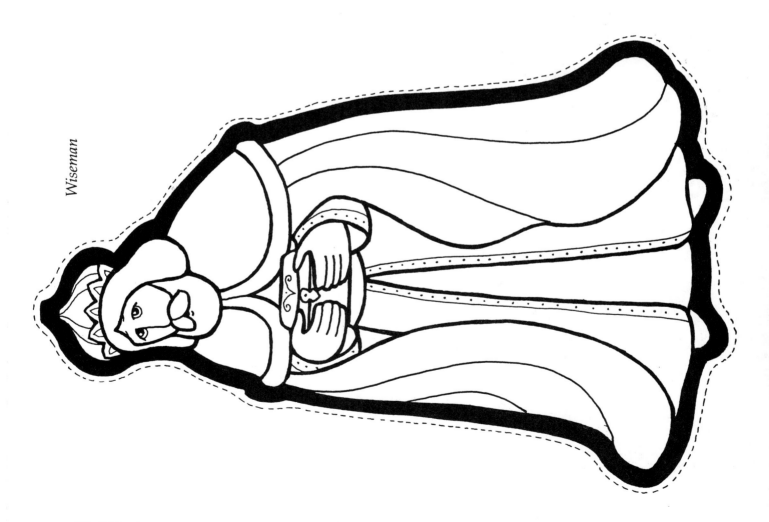

Soldier

King Herod

Soldier

Priest

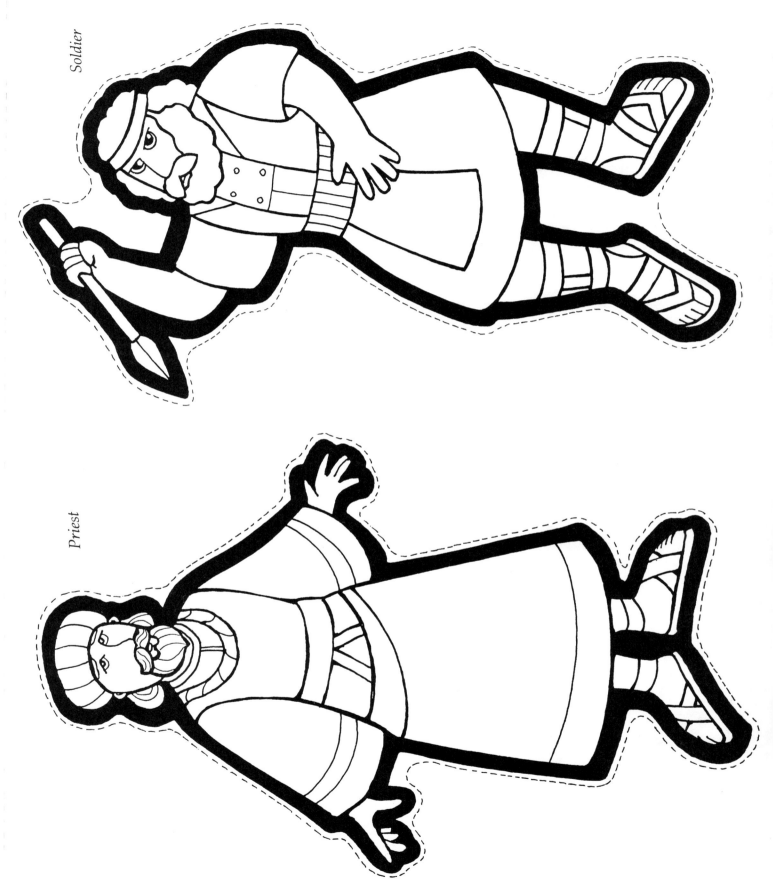

Jesus, age 12

Old Priest

20

Jesus, as Adult (Smiling)

John the Baptist

IF9699 New Testament Bible Story Patterns

Satan

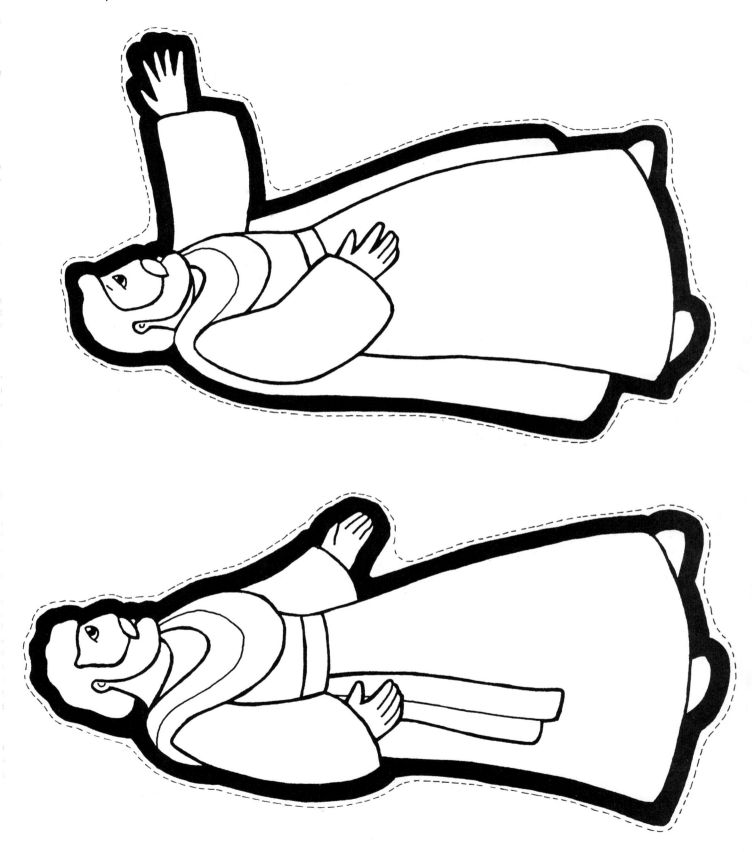

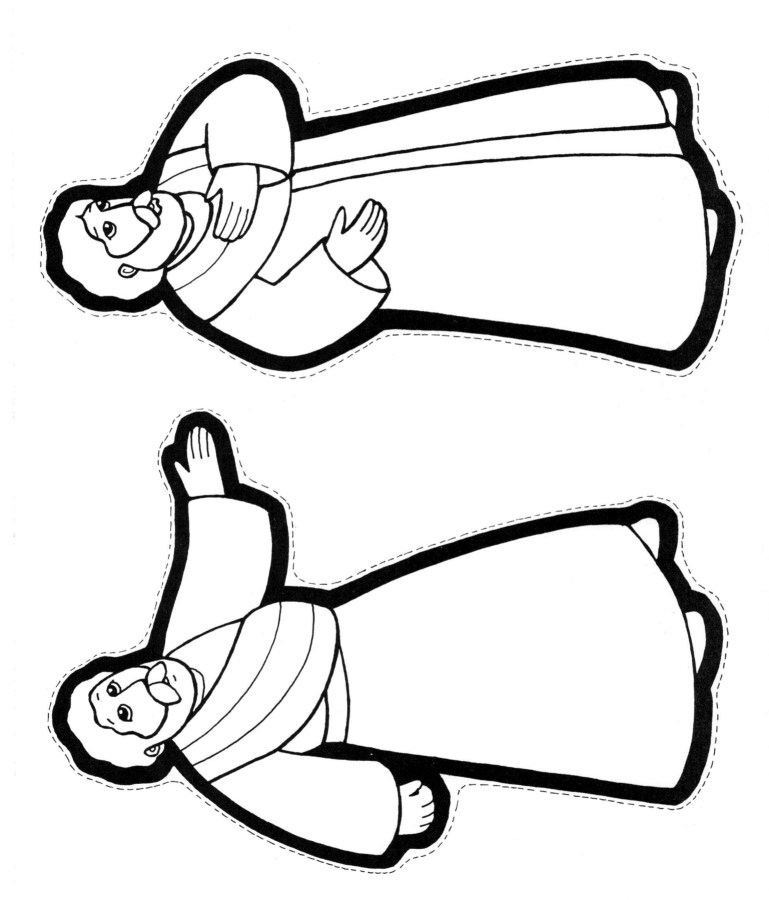

Bridegroom

Mary (older)

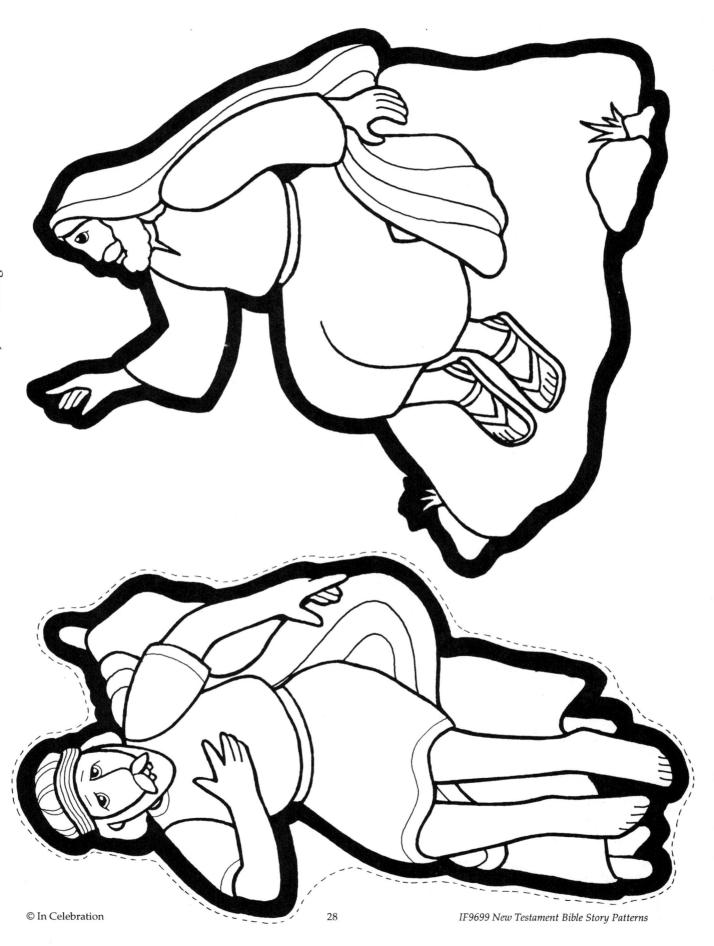

Jesus Sitting

Man on Stretcher

IF9699 New Testament Bible Story Patterns

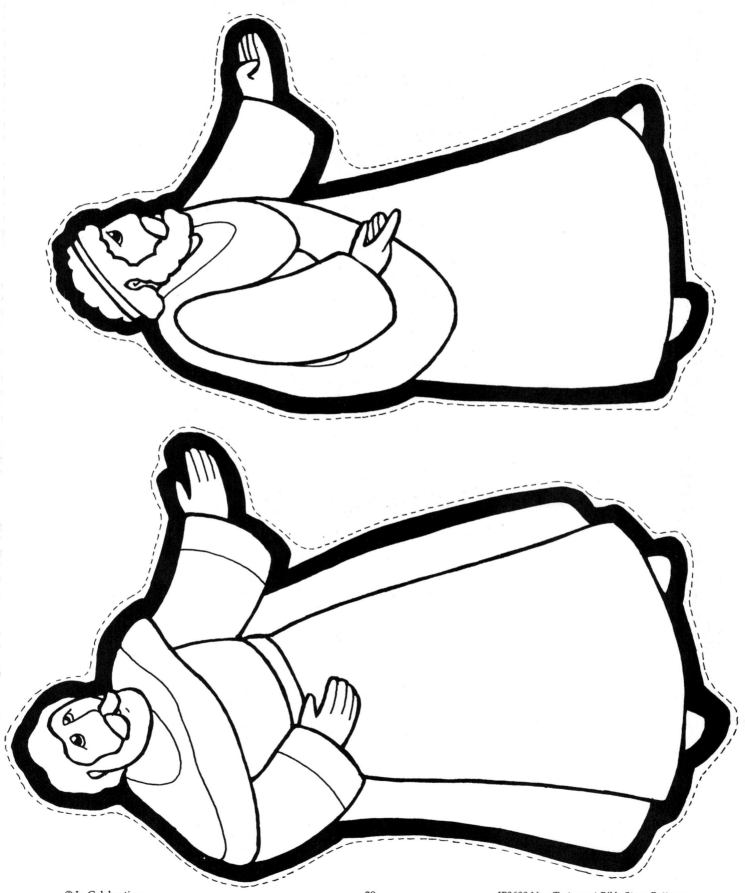

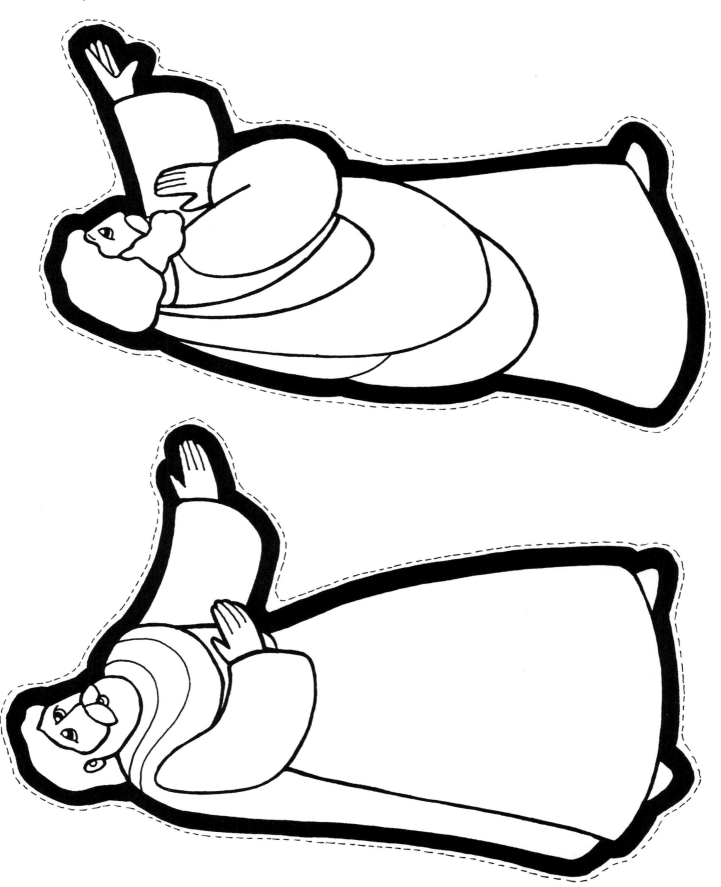

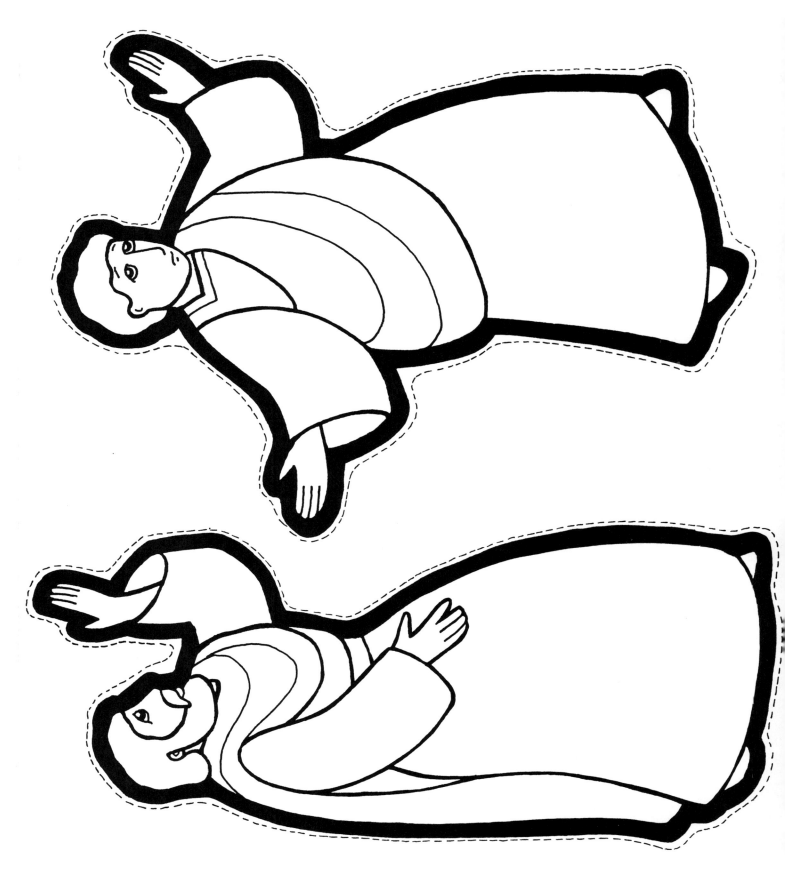

31

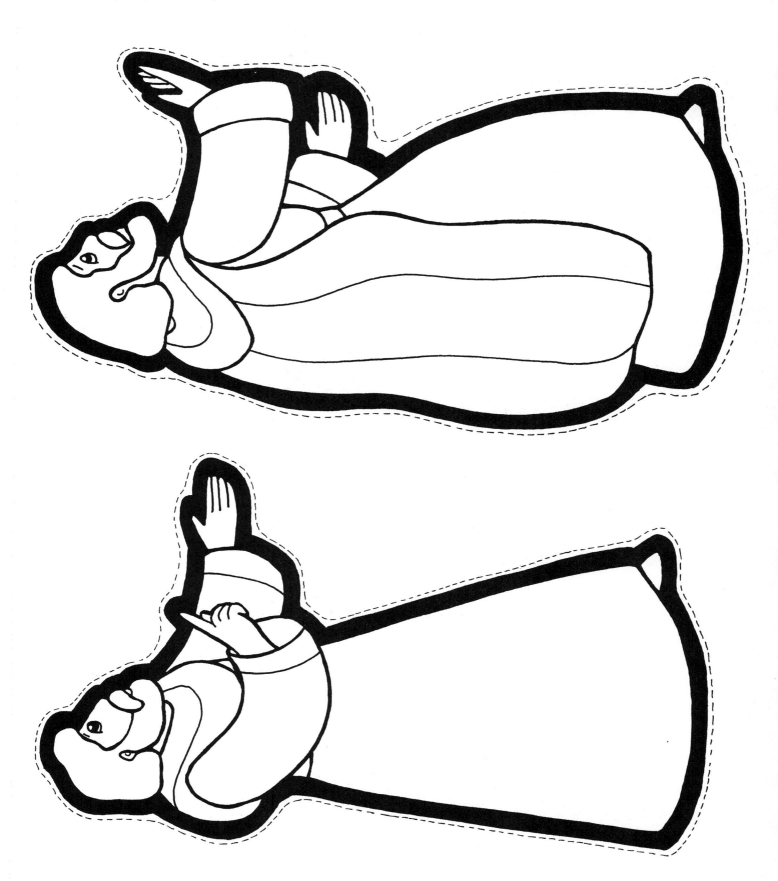

Simon the Pharisee

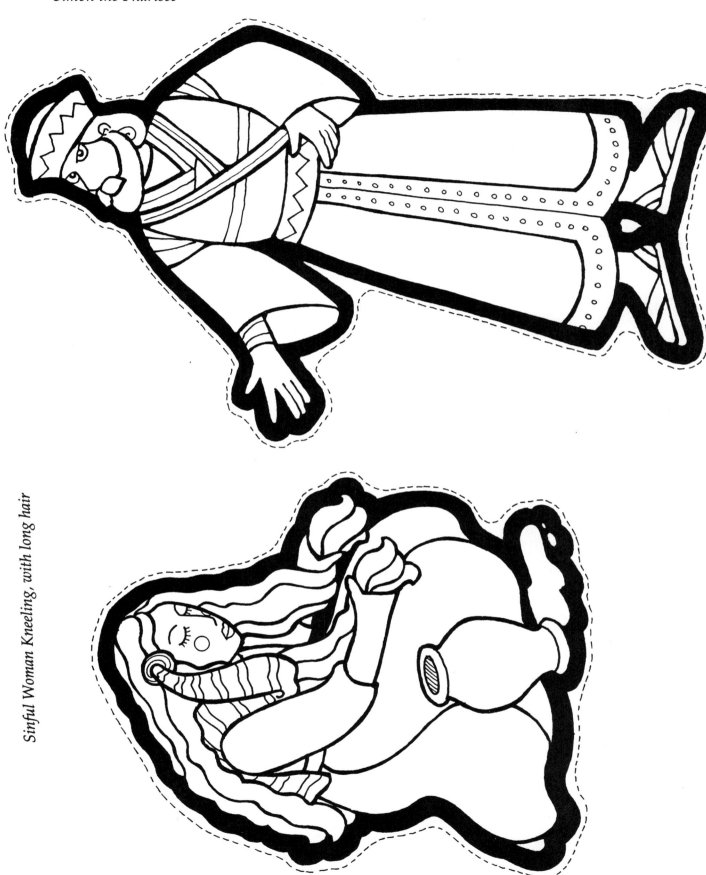

Sinful Woman Kneeling, with long hair

IF9699 New Testament Bible Story Patterns

2 Crippled People Sitting

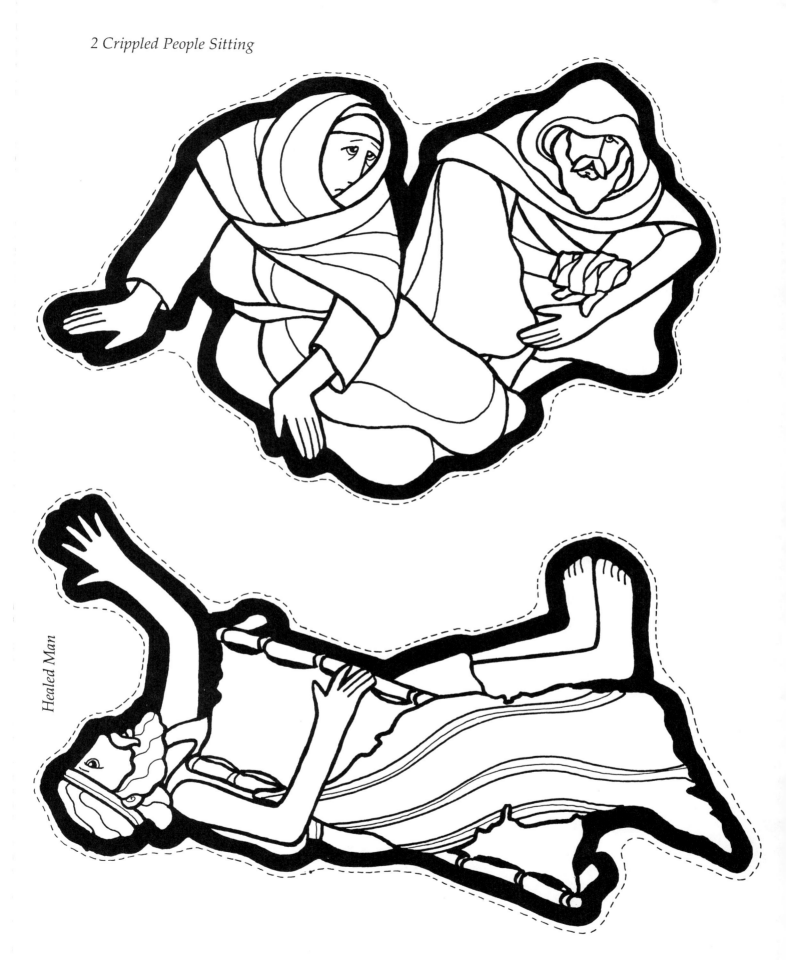

Healed Man

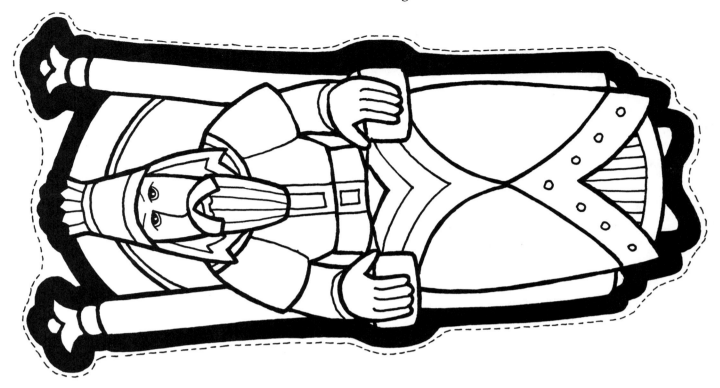

Blind Man (Make 2)

Little Boy with 5 Loaves of Bread and 2 Fish

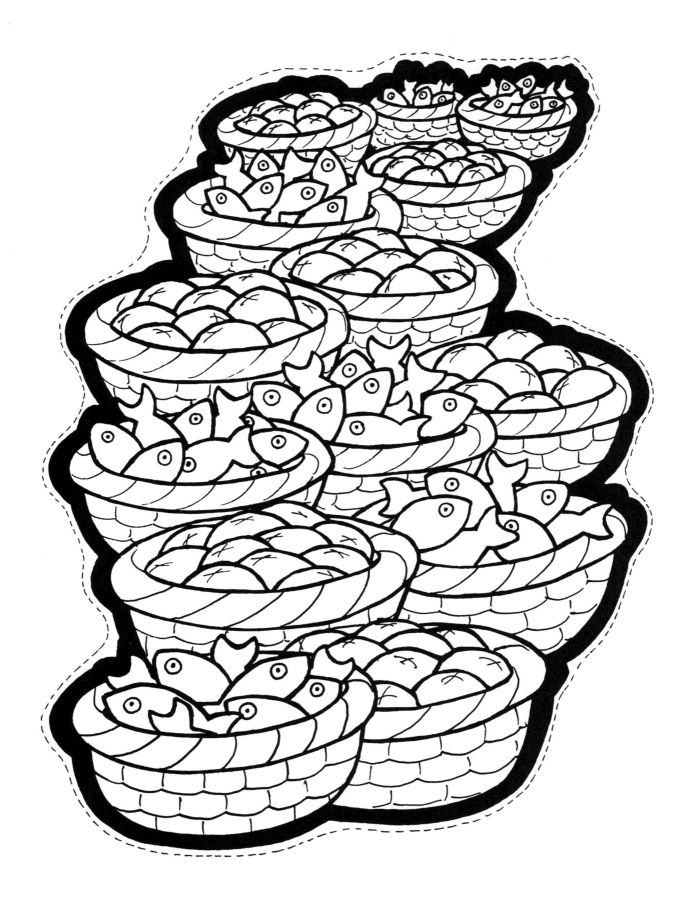

Nine Lepers in Group

44

One Leper

45

Injured Man

Robber

46

IF9699 New Testament Bible Story Patterns

Religious Leader

Robber

Good Samaritan

Innkeeper

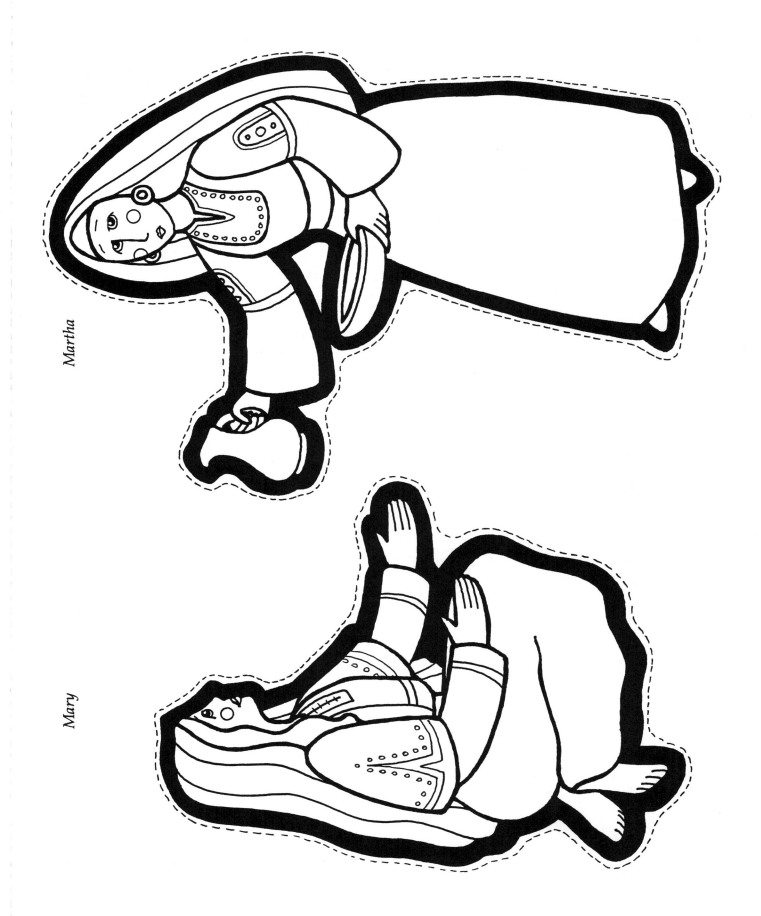

Martha

Mary

Lazarus

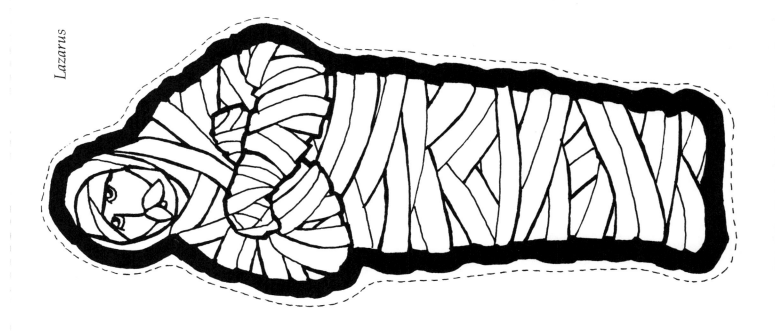

Young Prodigal Son

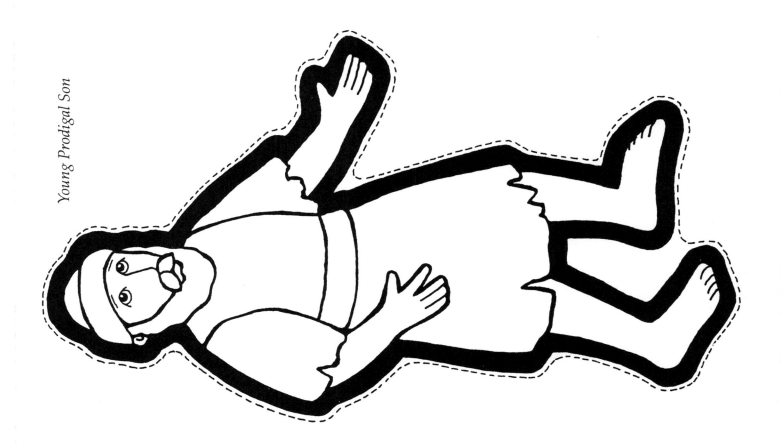

Older Son

Father of Prodigal Son

Group of Children

52

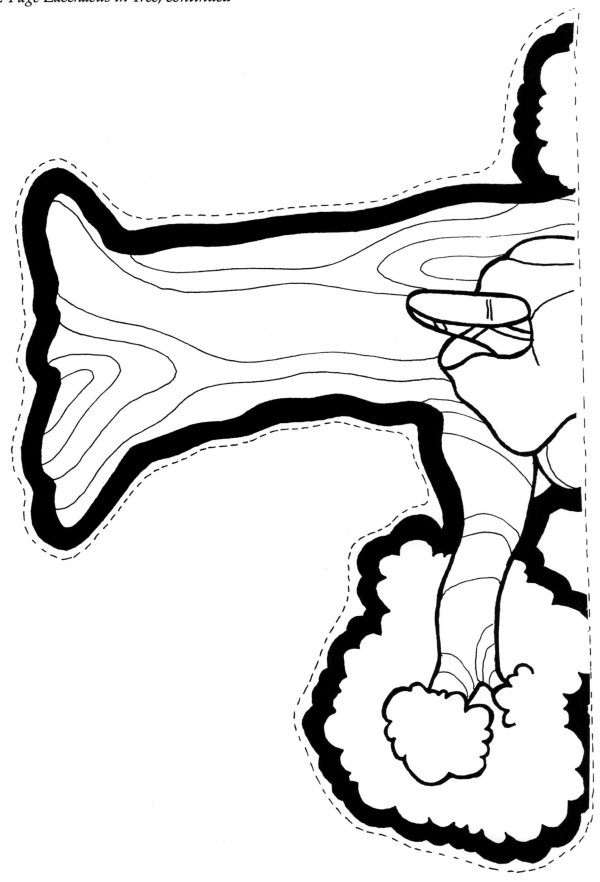

Happy Crowd Cheering

55

56

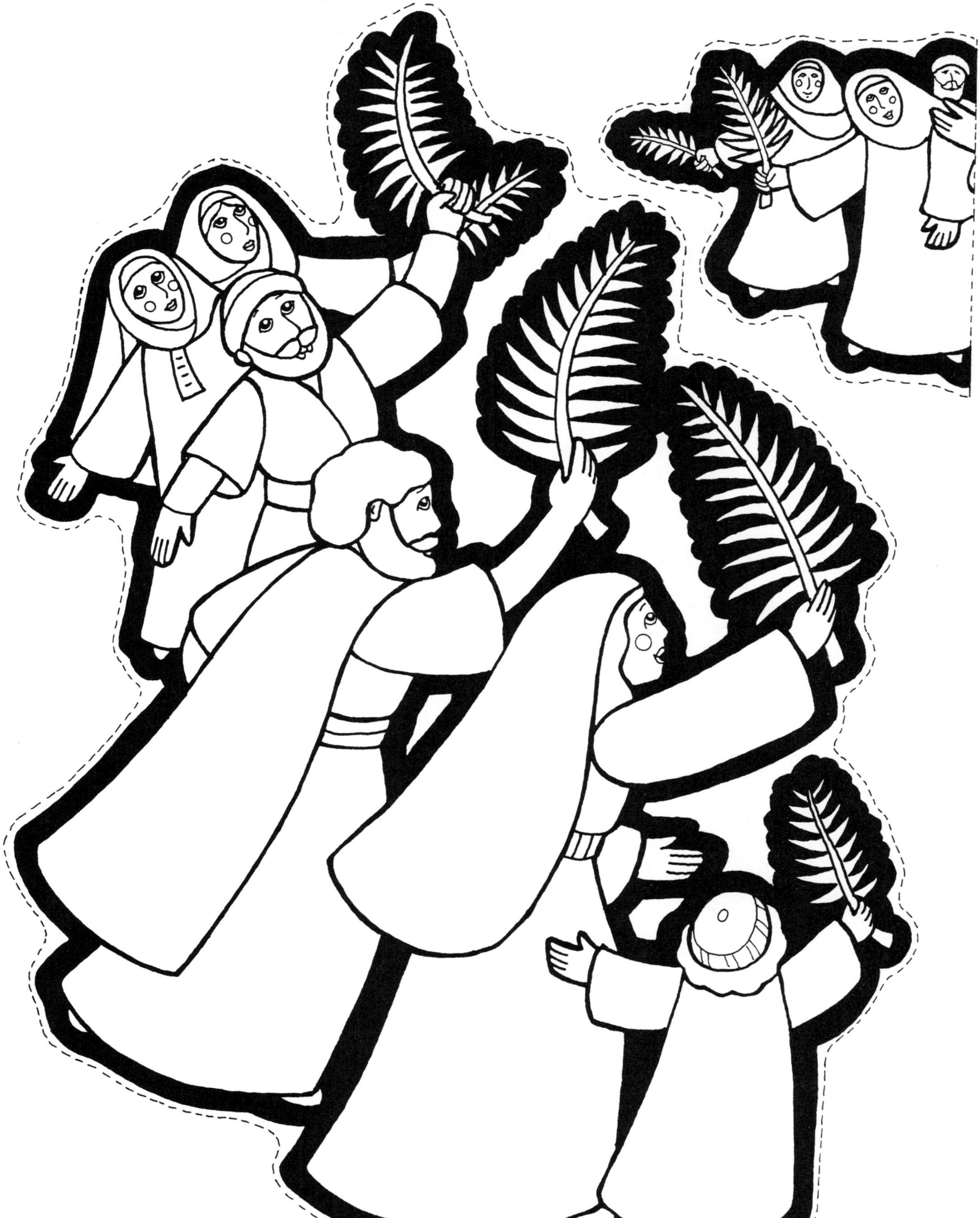

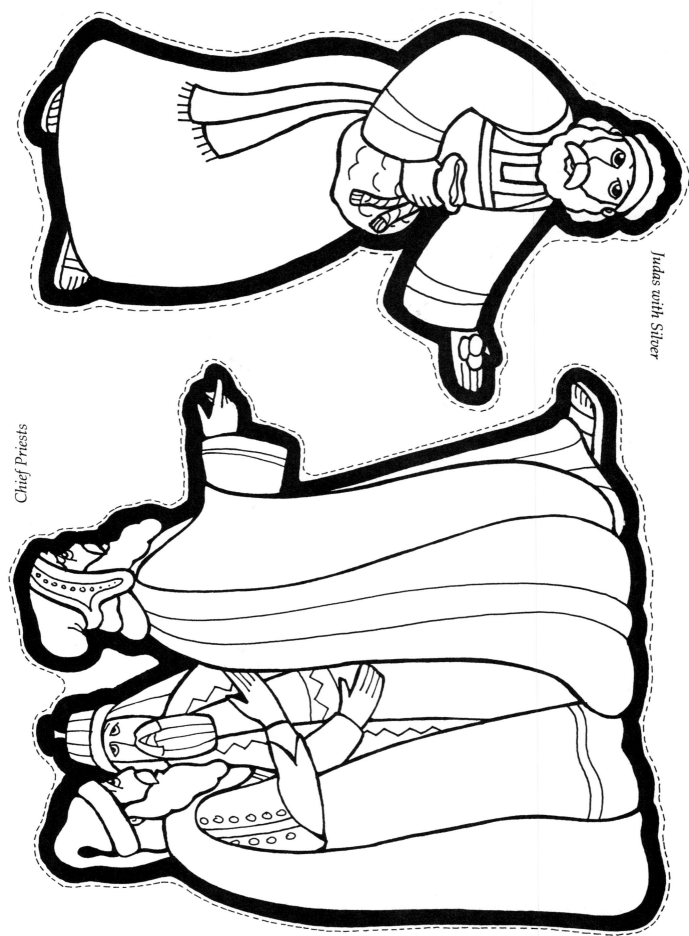

Judas with Silver

Chief Priests

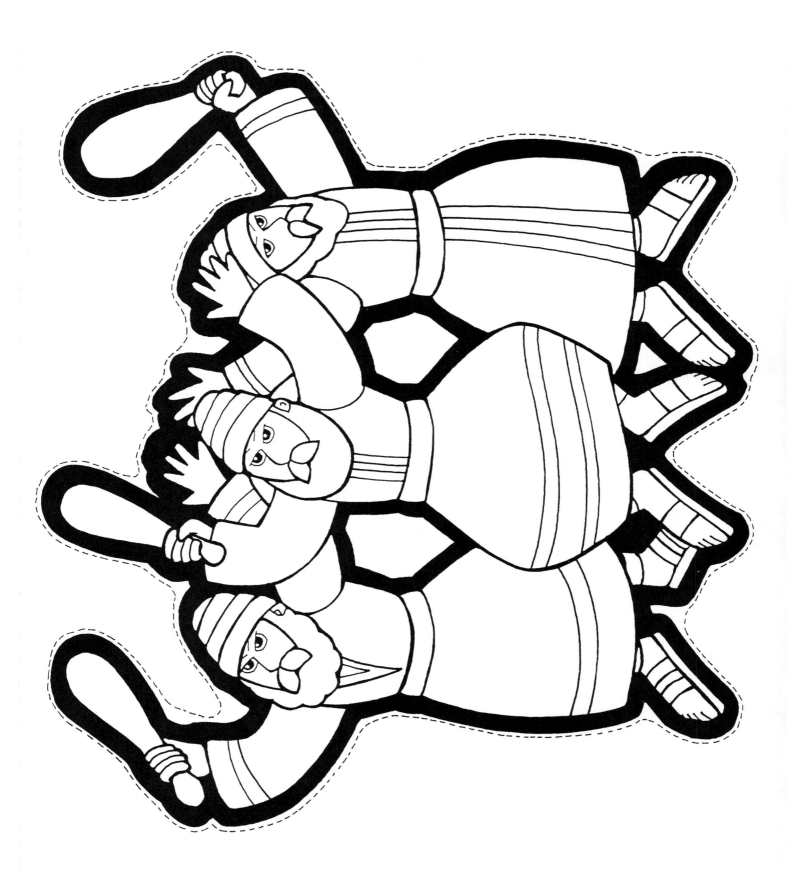

Girl

Peter Sitting by the Fire

72

Girl

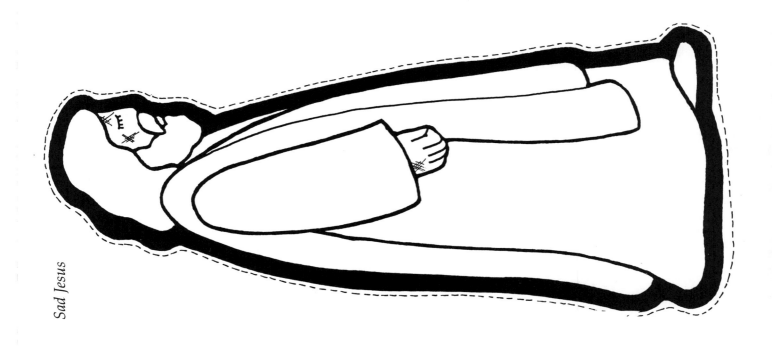

Sad Jesus

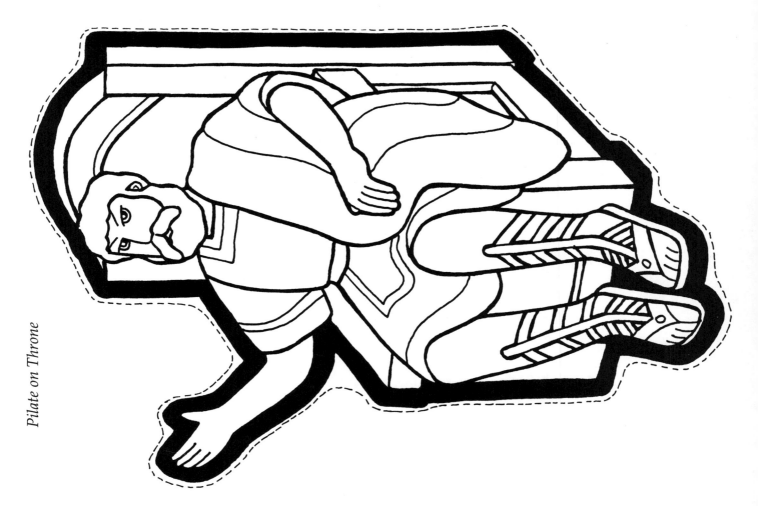

Pilate on Throne

Barabbas

Herod

Jesus with Crown of Thorns

Cross

Jesus on Cross

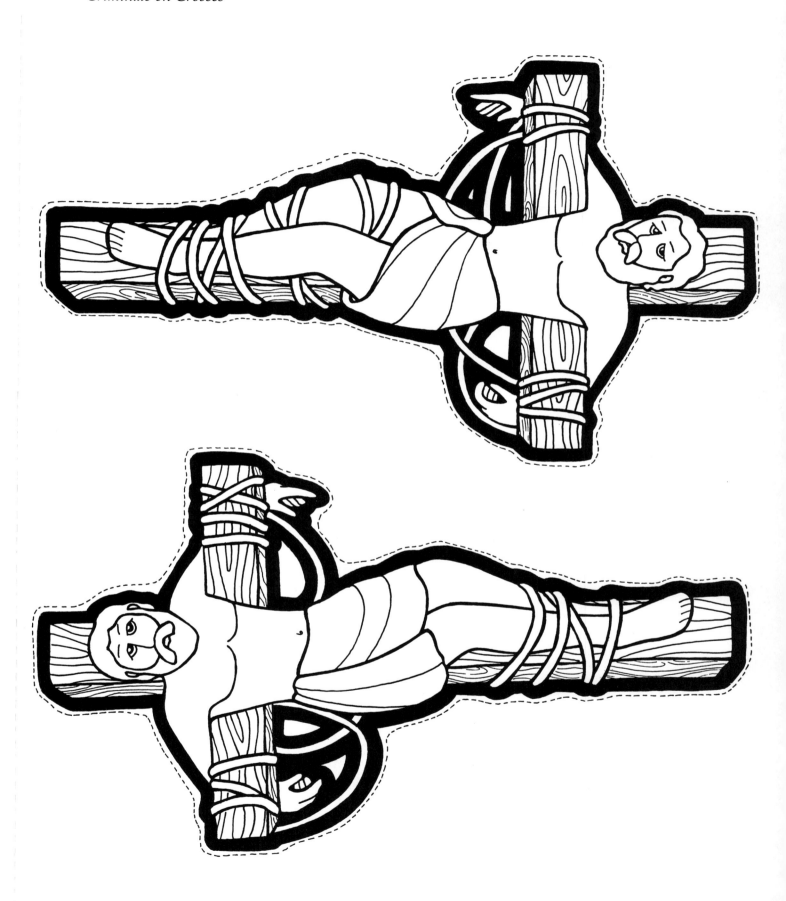

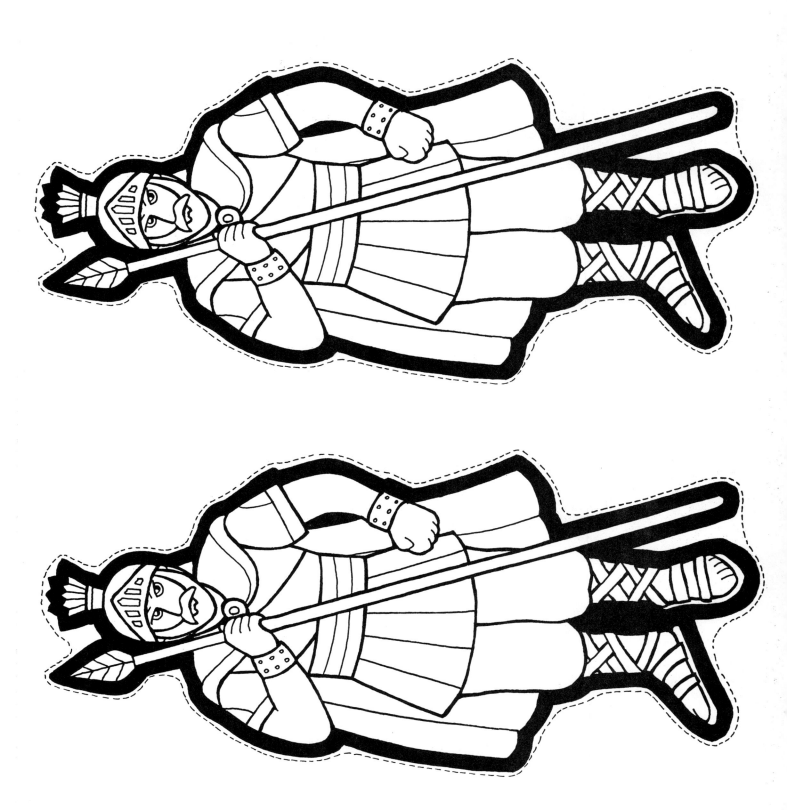

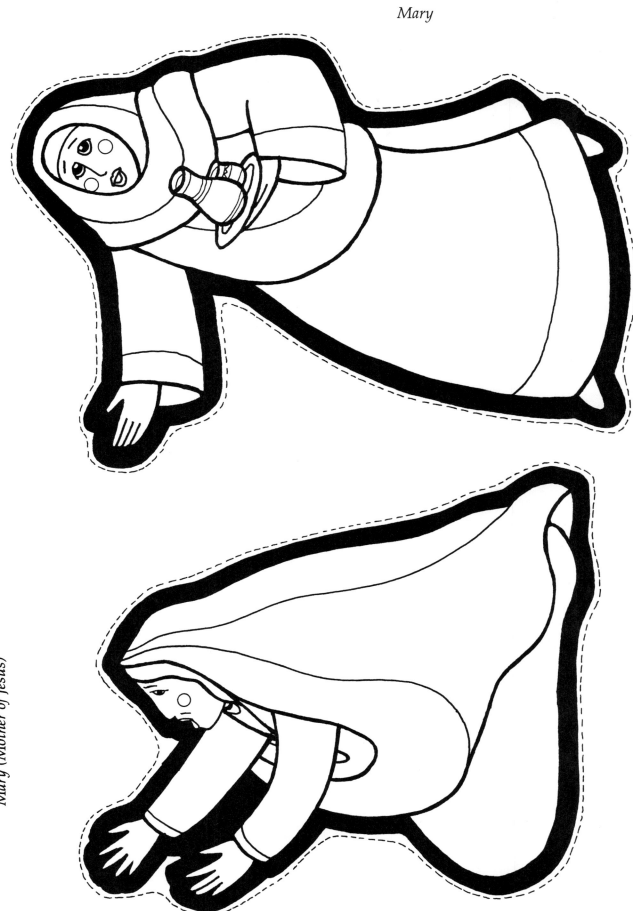

Mary (Mother of Jesus)

Mary Magdalene

Angel

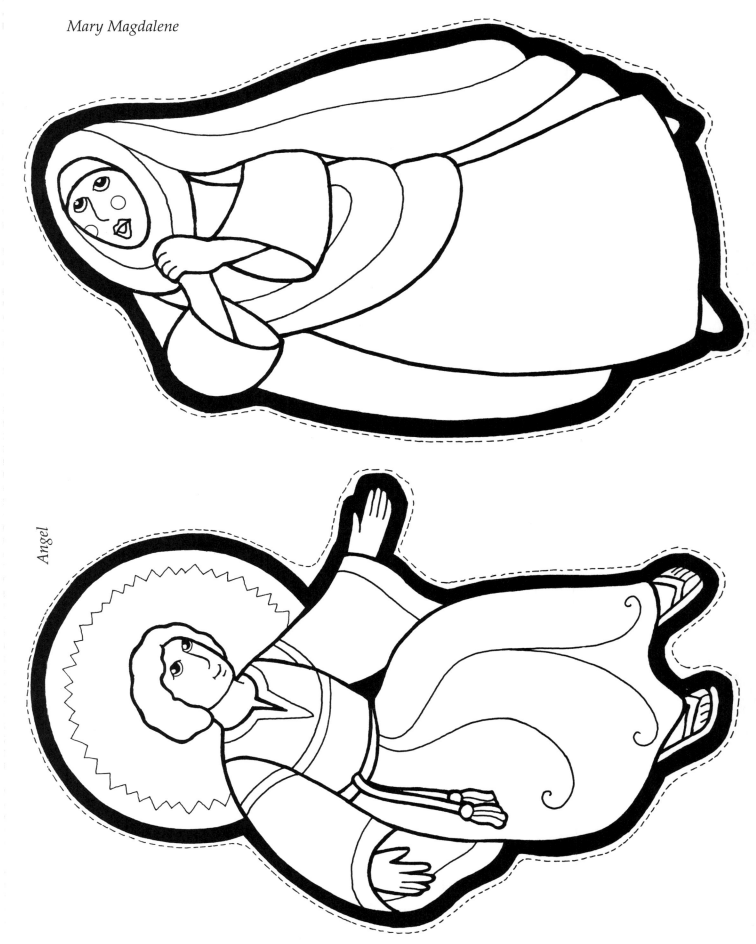

IF9699 New Testament Bible Story Patterns

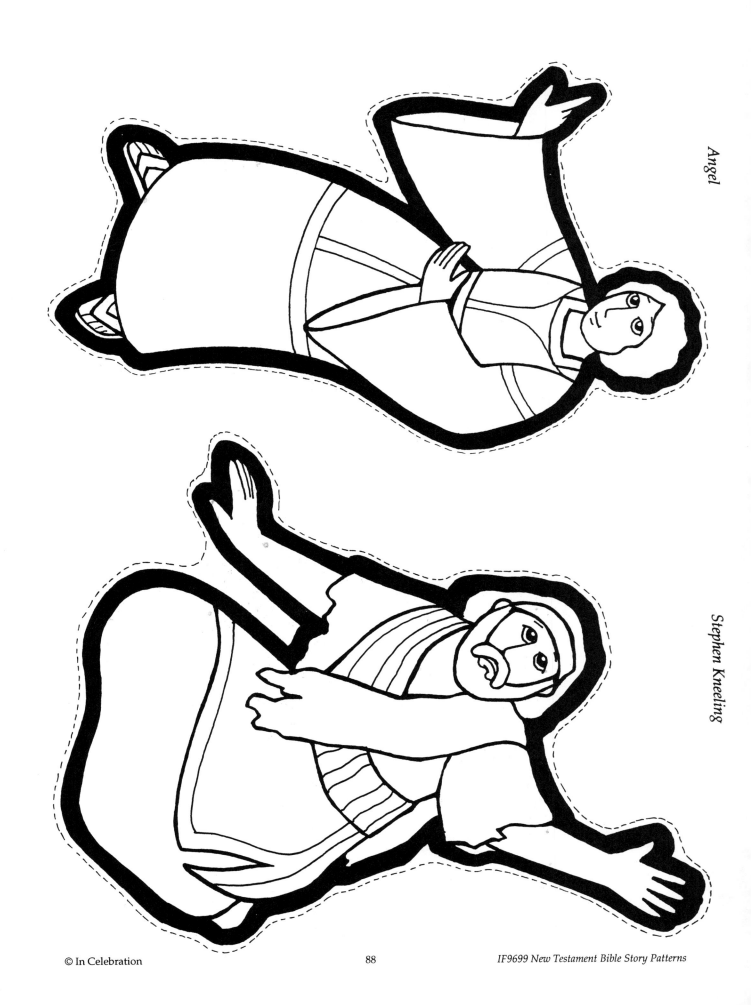

Angel

Stephen Kneeling

IF9699 New Testament Bible Story Patterns

Crowd of People

89

IF9699 New Testament Bible Story Patterns

Saul Blinded

2 Friends

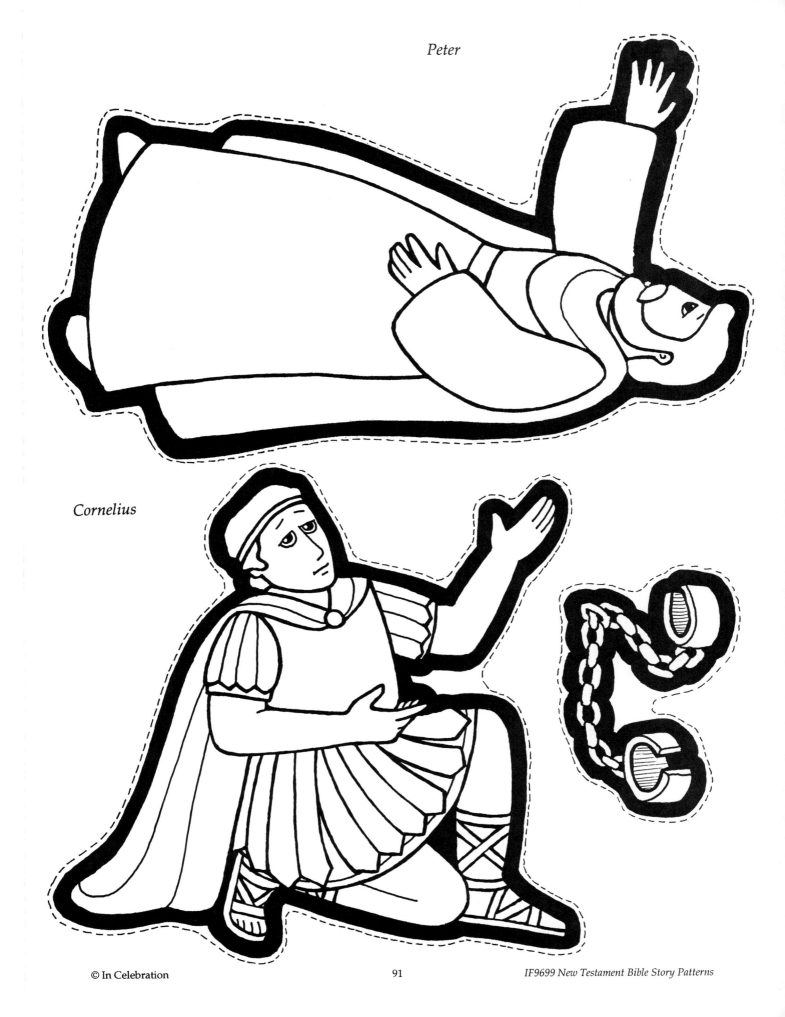

Peter

Cornelius

Standing, Sleeping Guard

Angel

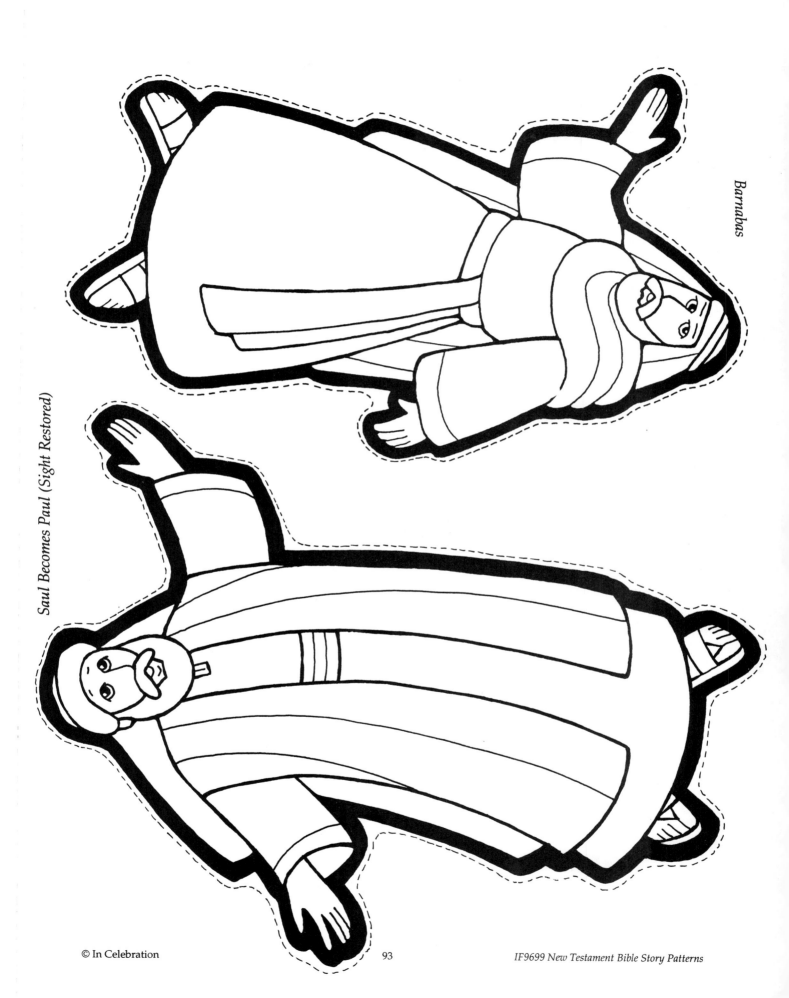

Barnabas

Saul Becomes Paul (Sight Restored)

Same Man Healed (Able to Walk)

Crippled Man

Silas and Paul in Chains

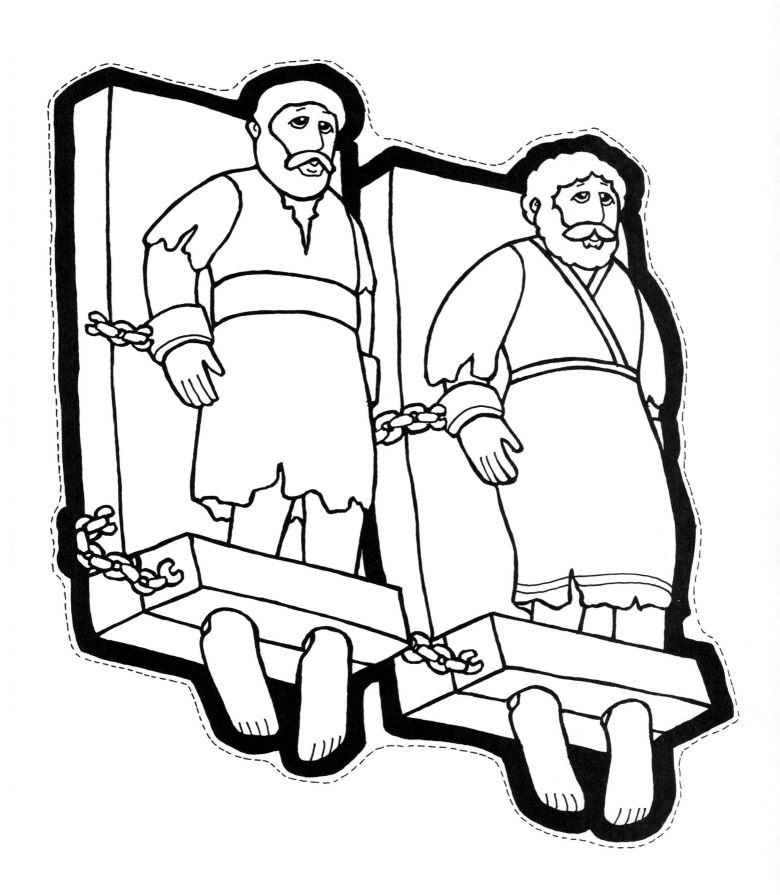

Commander

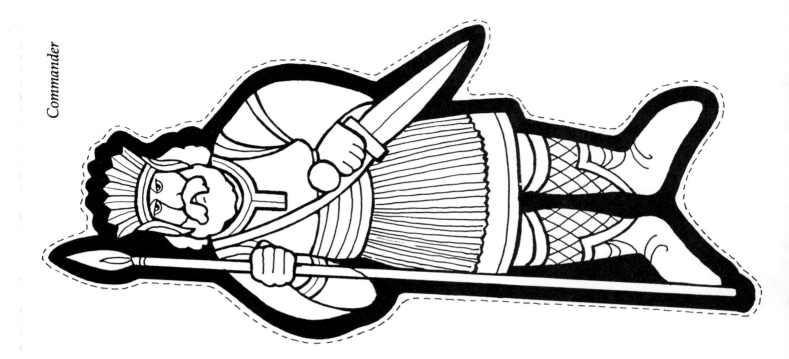

Older Paul

Angry Crowd

IF9699 New Testament Bible Story Patterns

King Agrippa

Festas (Roman Governor)

Paul Writing in a Rome Prison

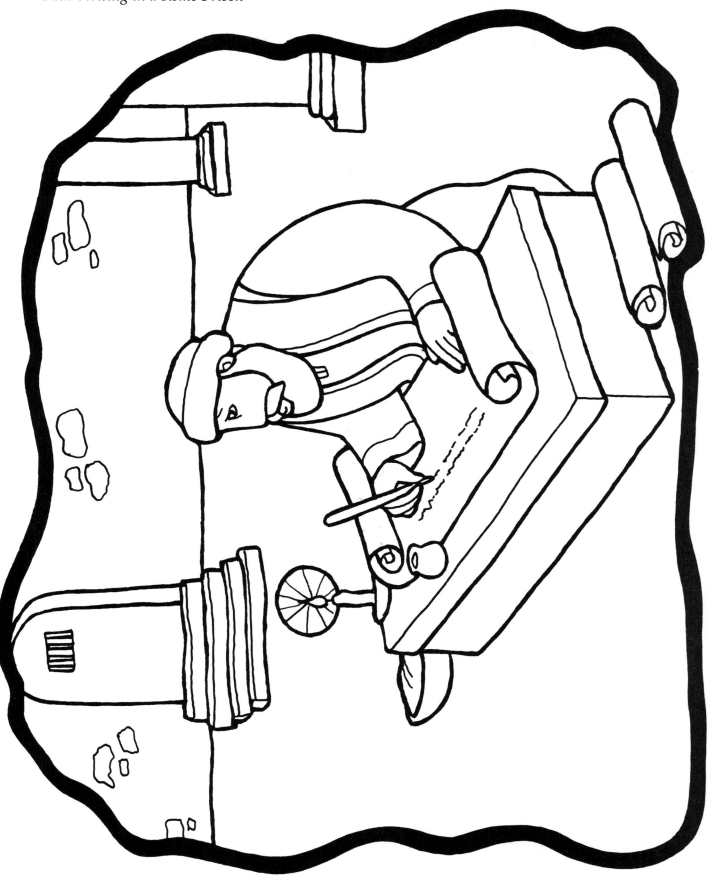

Donkey

Sheep

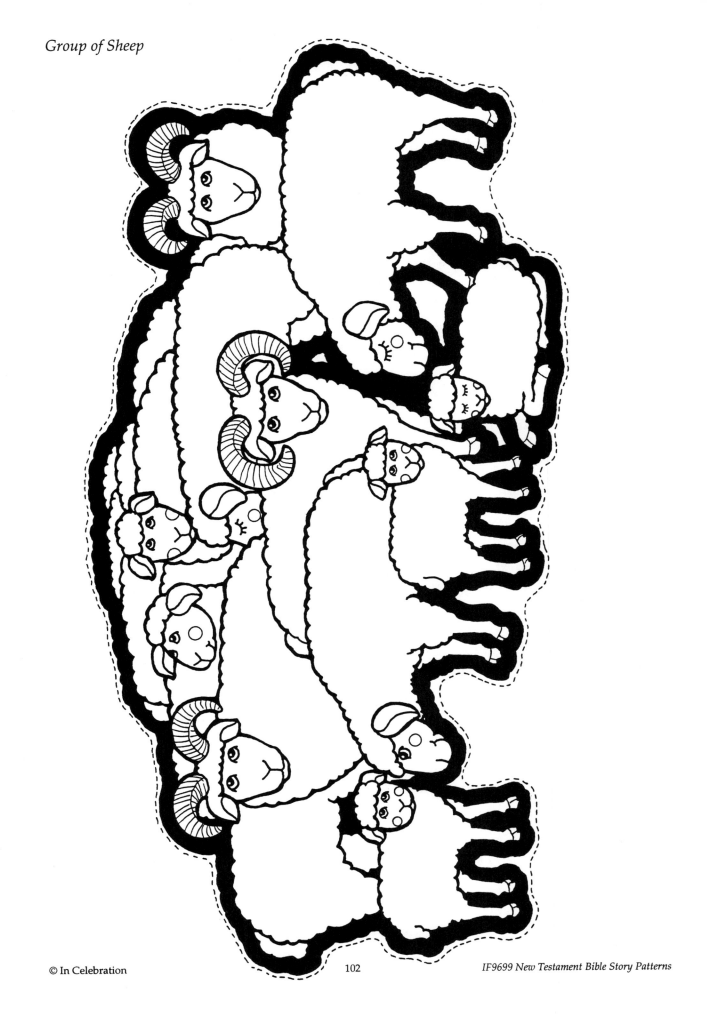

2 Doves

Ram

Cow

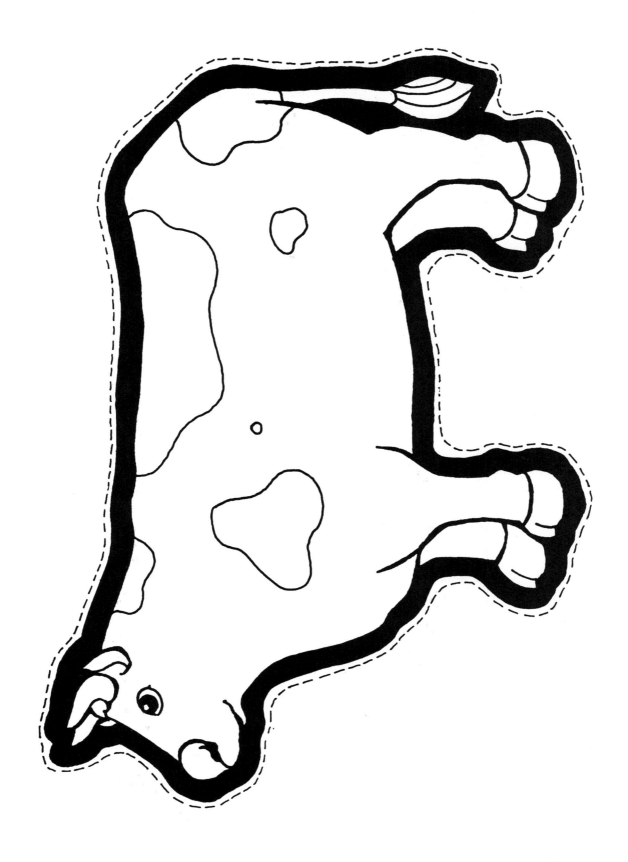

2-Page Camel with Packs

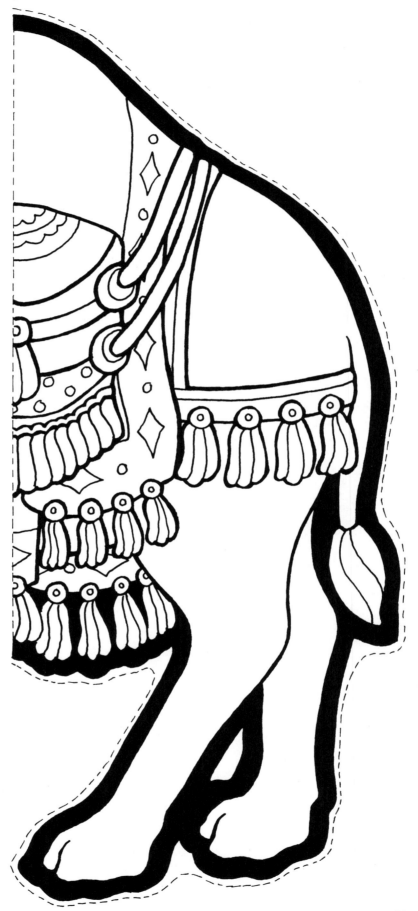

Crow on Pedestal

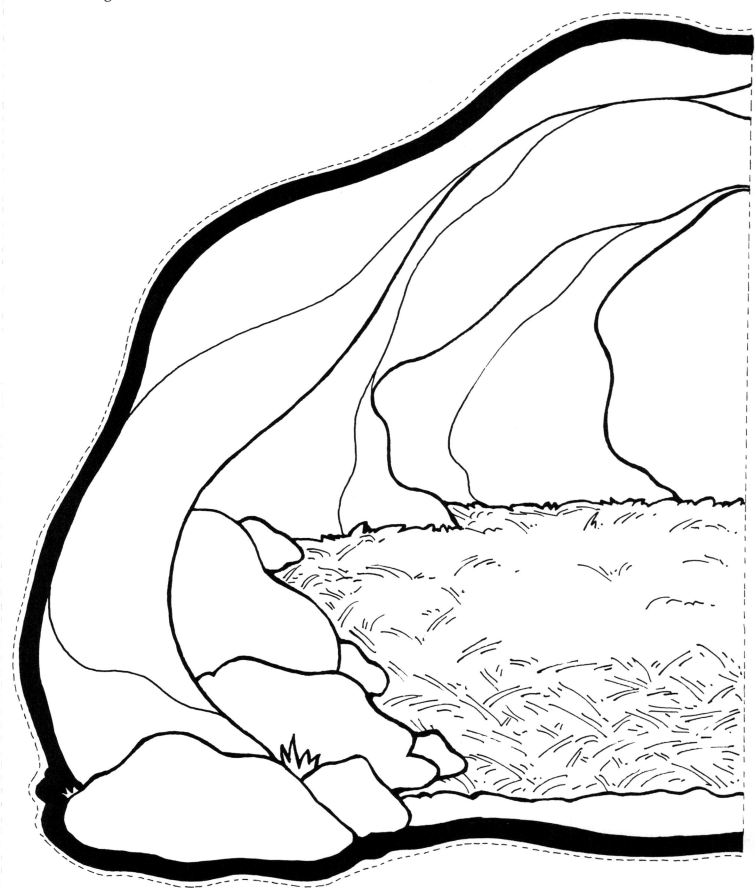

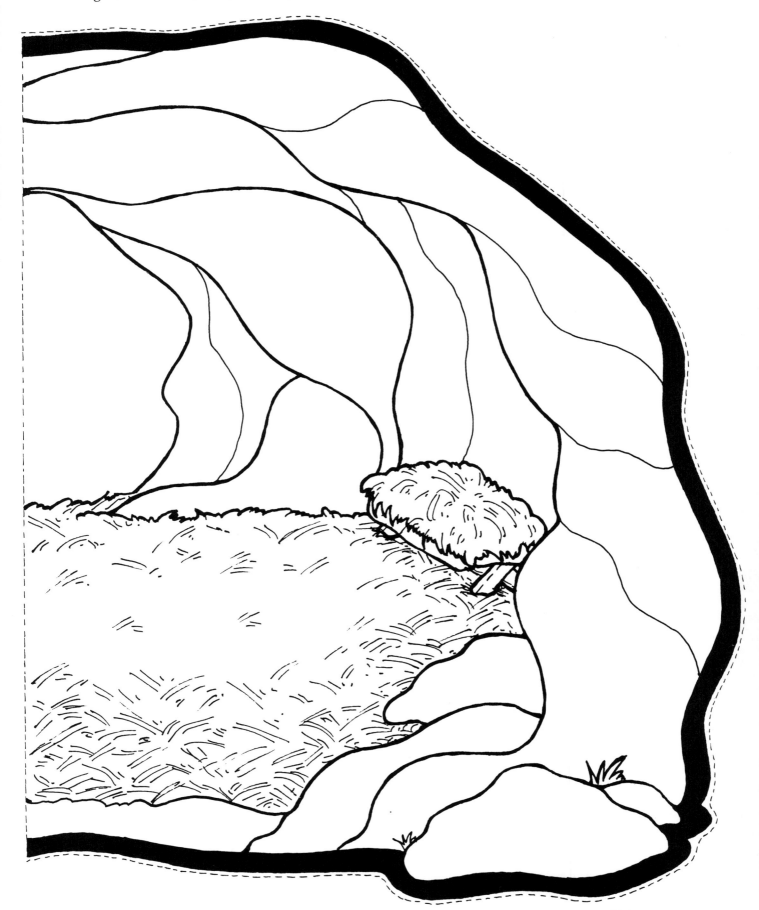

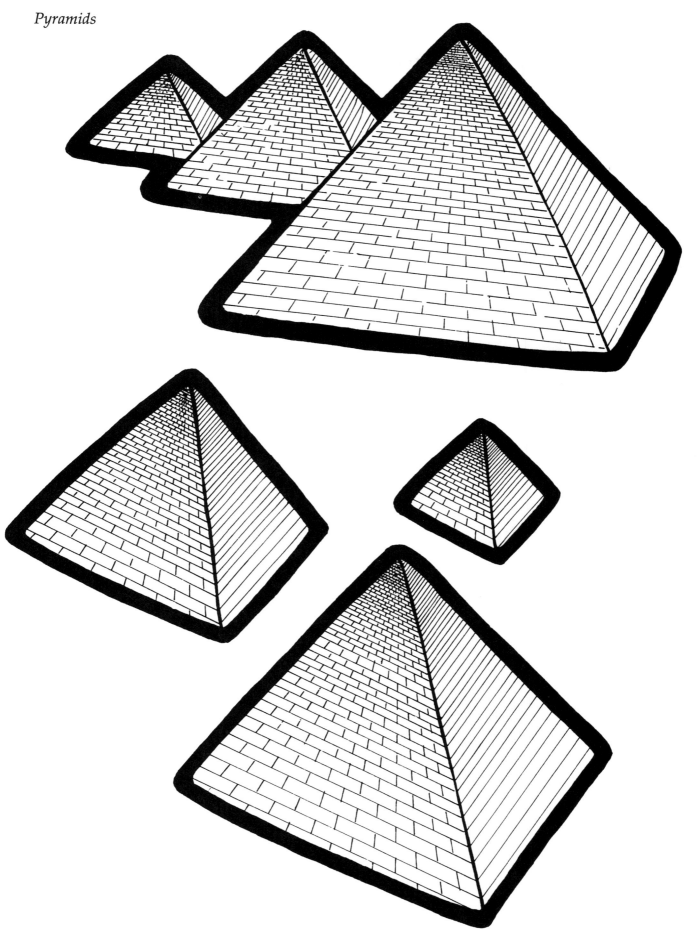

2-Page Jordan River Scene

2-Page Fishing Boat

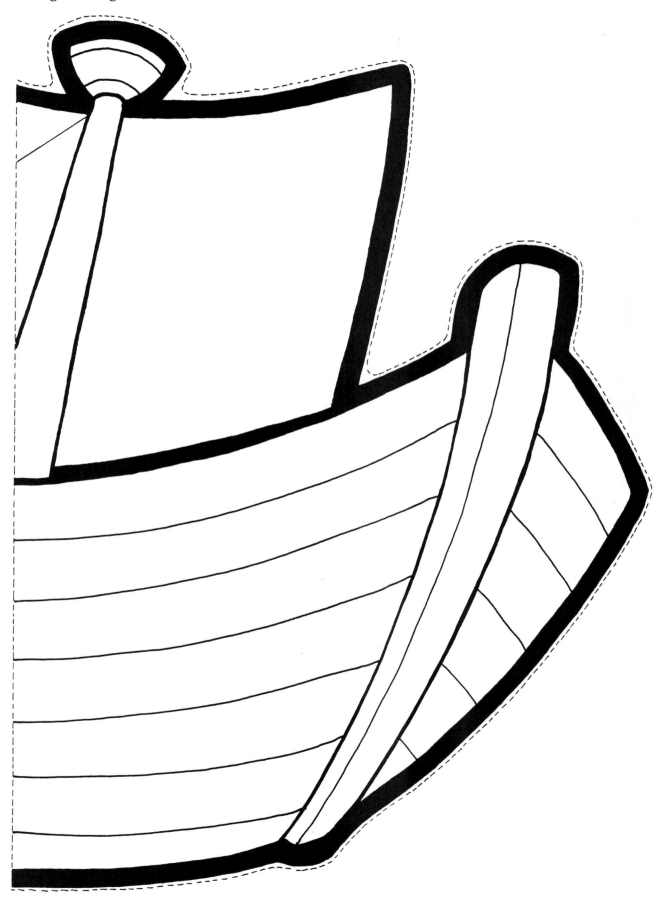

Well

129

Trees/Flowers

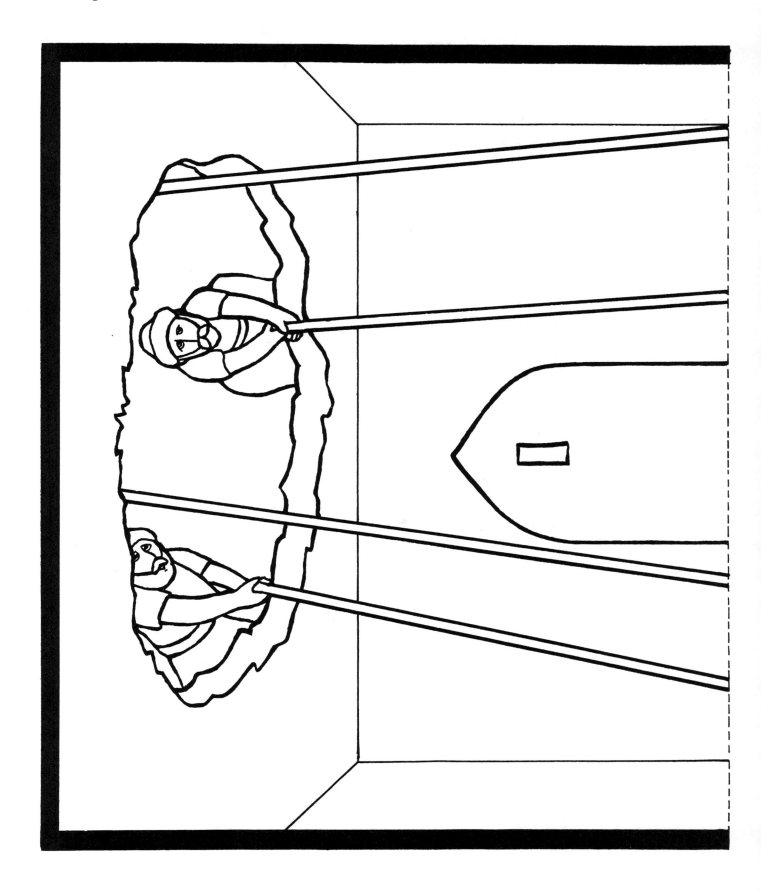

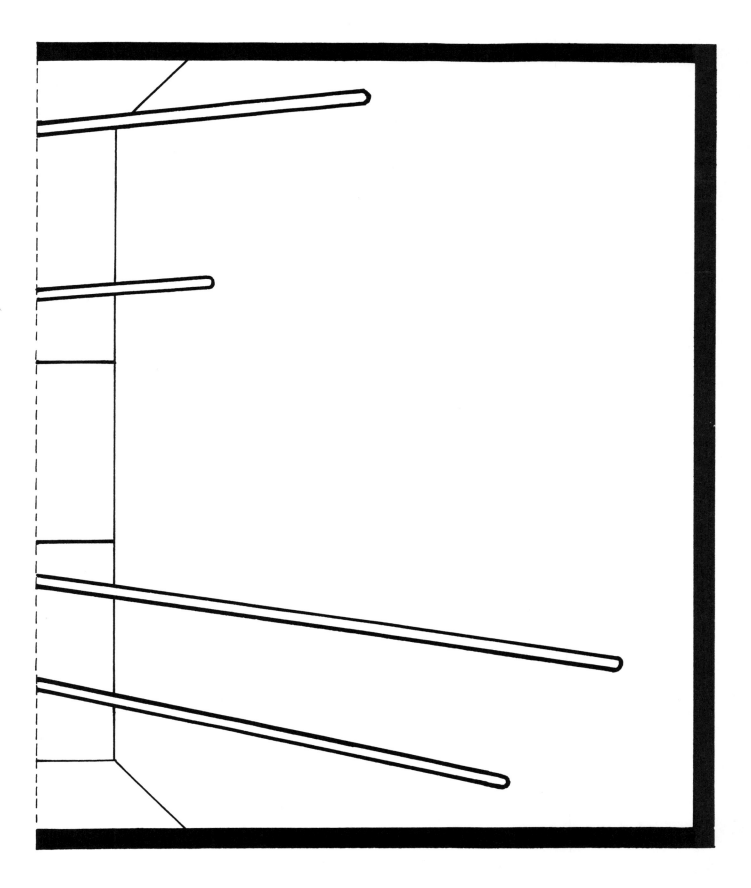

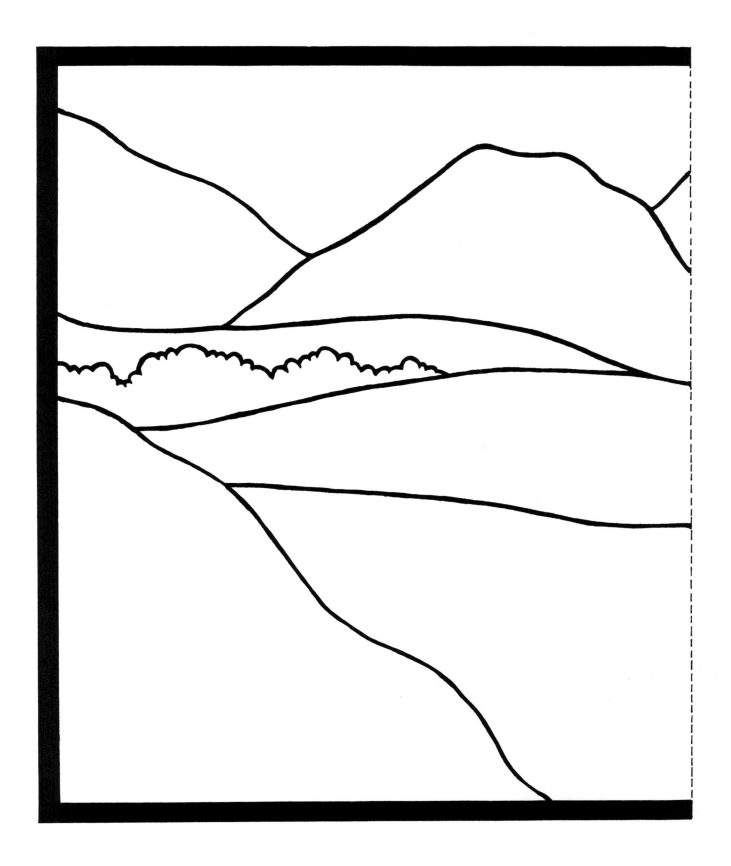

3-Page Hillside with Many People

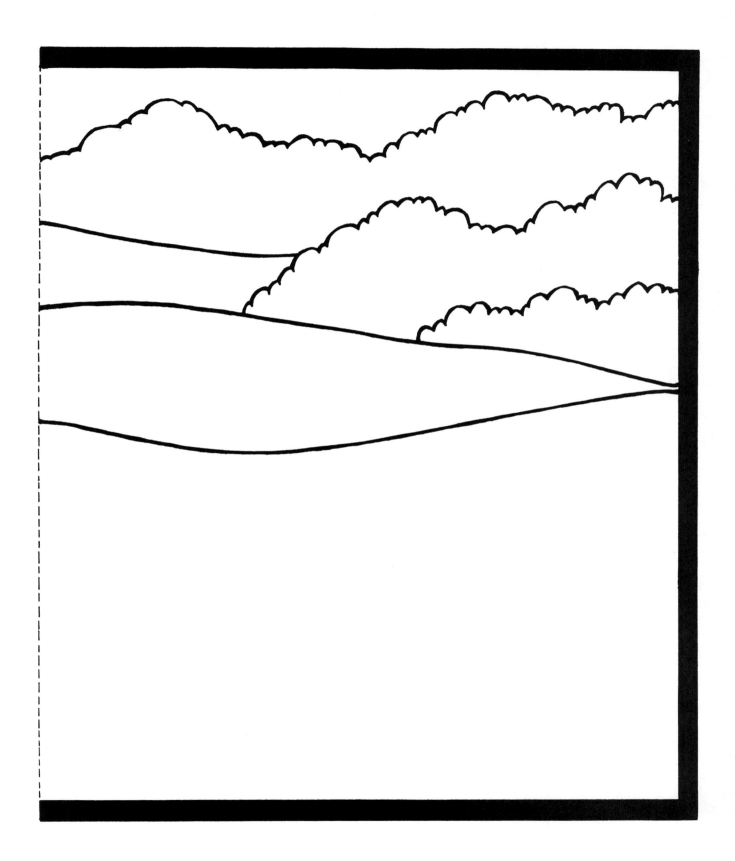

2-*Page Pool Scene, continued*

The Beatitudes

Blessed are the poor in spirit,
for theirs is the kingdom of heaven.

Blessed are those who mourn,
for they will be comforted.

Blessed are the meek,
for they will inherit the earth.

Blessed are those who hunger and thirst
for righteousness,
for they will be filled.

Blessed are the merciful,
for they will be shown mercy.

Blessed are the pure in heart,
for they will see God.

Blessed are the peacemakers,
for they will be called sons of God.

Blessed are those who are persecuted
because of righteousness,
for theirs is the kingdom of heaven.

Blessed are you when people insult
you, persecute you and falsely say all
kinds of evil against you because of me.
Rejoice and be glad, because great is
your reward in heaven, for in the same
way they persecuted the prophets who
were before you.

The Lord's Prayer

Our Father who art in heaven,
hallowed be thy name,
thy kingdom come,
thy will be done,
on earth as it is in heaven.
Give us this day our daily bread,
and forgive us our trespasses,
as we forgive those
who trespass against us,
and lead us not into temptation,
but deliver us from evil.
For thine is the kingdom
and the power and the glory
forever and ever.   Amen

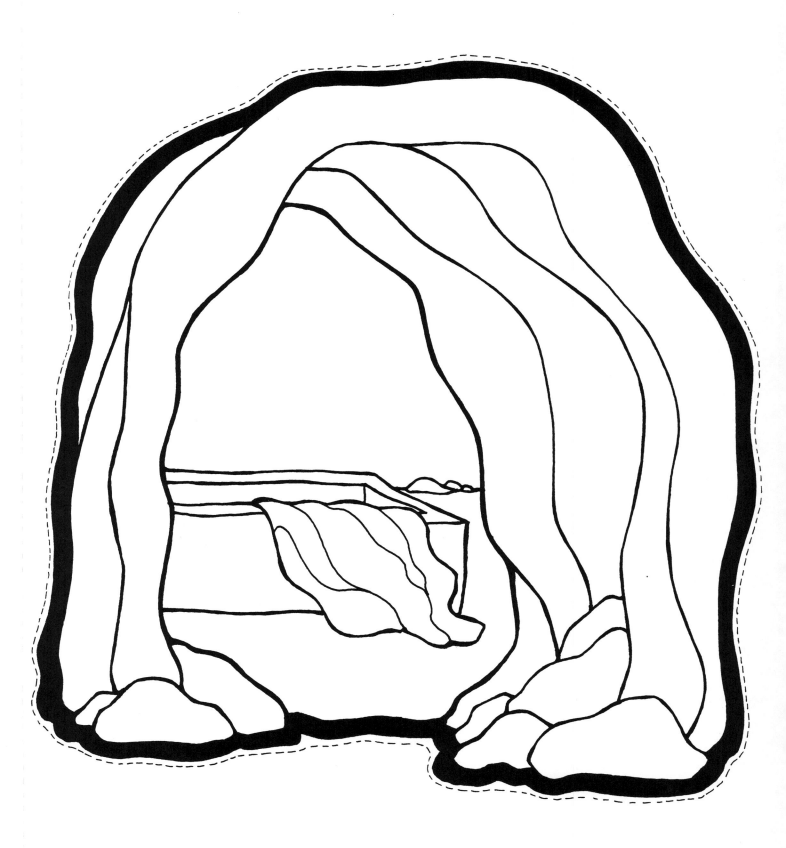

All 12 Disciples Standing in a Group

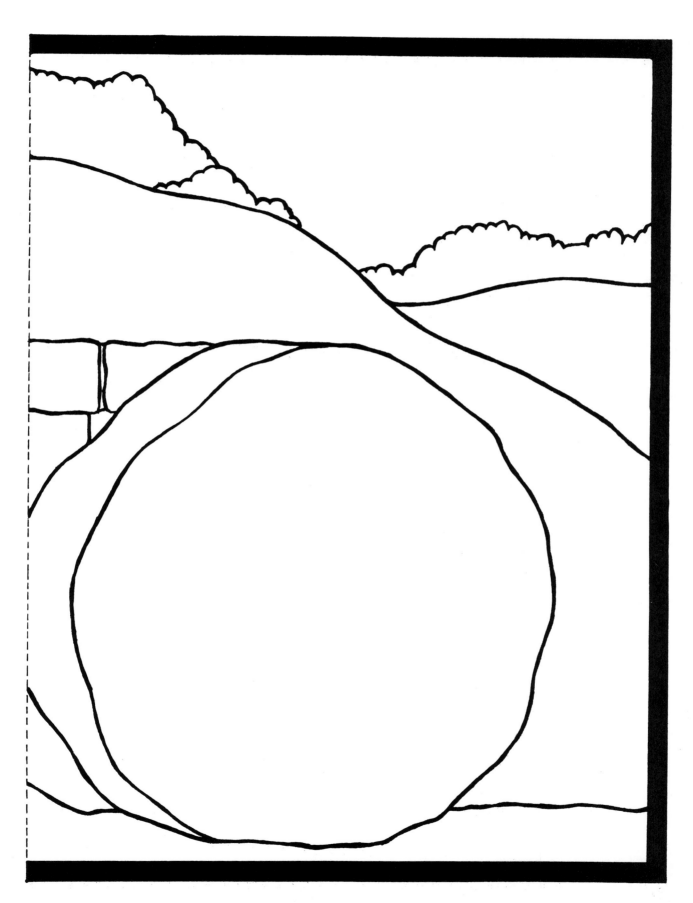

2-Page Inside of Home